THOMAS MERTON

MODERN SPIRITUAL MASTERS
Robert Ellsberg, Series Editor

This series introduces the writing and vision of some of the great spiritual masters of the twentieth century. Along with selections from their writings, each volume includes a comprehensive introduction, presenting the author's life and writings in context and drawing attention to points of special relevance to contemporary spirituality.

Some of these authors found a wide audience in their lifetimes. In other cases recognition has come long after their deaths. Some are rooted in long-established traditions of spirituality. Others charted new, untested paths. In each case, however, the authors in this series have engaged in a spiritual journey shaped by the influences and concerns of our age. Such concerns include the challenges of modern science, religious pluralism, secularism, and the quest for social justice.

At the dawn of a new millennium this series commends these modern spiritual masters, along with the saints and witnesses of previous centuries, as guides and companions to a new generation of seekers.

Already published:
Dietrich Bonhoeffer (edited by Robert Coles)
Simone Weil (edited by Eric O. Springsted)
Henri Nouwen (edited by Robert A. Jonas)
Pierre Teilhard de Chardin (edited by Ursula King)
Charles de Foucauld (edited by Robert Ellsberg)
Oscar Romero (by Marie Dennis, Rennie Golden,
   and Scott Wright)
Eberhard Arnold (edited by Johann Christoph Arnold)
Forthcoming volumes include:
Thich Nhat Hanh
Flannery O'Connor
Edith Stein
G. K. Chesterton

THOMAS MERTON

Essential Writings

Selected
with an Introduction by

CHRISTINE M.
BOCHEN

ORBIS BOOKS

Maryknoll, New York 10545

Founded in 1970, Orbis Books endeavors to publish works that enlighten the mind, nourish the spirit, and challenge the conscience. The publishing arm of the Maryknoll Fathers and Brothers, Orbis seeks to explore the global dimensions of the Christian faith and mission, to invite dialogue with diverse cultures and religious traditions, and to serve the cause of reconciliation and peace. The books published reflect the views of their authors and do not represent the official position of the Maryknoll Society. To learn more about Maryknoll and Orbis Books, please visit our website at www.maryknollsociety.org.

Published by Orbis Books, Maryknoll, NY 10545-0308

Page 9 represents an extension of the copyright page.

Manufactured in the United States of America

Library of Congress Cataloging-in-Publication Data

Merton, Thomas, 1915-1968.
    [Selections. English. 2000]
    Thomas Merton / writings selected with an introduction by Christine
M. Bochen.
        p.   cm. – (Modern spiritual masters series)
    Includes bibliographical references.
    ISBN 1-57075-331-8
    1. Christian life – Catholic authors. 2. Christianity and other
religions.
I. Bochen, Christine M.   II. Title.   III. Series.
BX4705.M542A25 2000
248.4'82 – dc21

                                                    00-051681

Contents

Sources

AJ   *The Asian Journal of Thomas Merton,* ed. Naomi Burton, Brother Patrick Hart, and James Laughlin (New York: New Directions, 1973)

CGB   *Conjectures of a Guilty Bystander* (New York: Doubleday, 1966)

CP   *The Collected Poems of Thomas Merton* (New York: New Directions, 1977)

CT   *The Courage for Truth: Letters to Writers,* ed. Christine M. Bochen (New York: Farrar, Straus & Giroux, 1993)

CWA   *Contemplation in a World of Action* (New York: Doubleday, 1971)

DQ   *Disputed Questions* (New York: Farrar, Straus & Cudahy, 1960)

DS   *Day of a Stranger,* ed. Robert E. Daggy (Salt Lake City: Gibbs M. Smith, 1981)

FV   *Faith and Violence* (Notre Dame, Ind.: University of Notre Dame Press, 1968)

HGL   *The Hidden Ground of Love: The Letters of Thomas Merton on Religious Experience and Social Concerns,* ed. William H. Shannon (New York: Farrar, Straus & Giroux, 1985)

HIR   *He Is Risen* (Niles, Ill.: Argus Communications, 1975)

HR   *"Honorable Reader": Reflections on My Work,* ed. Robert E. Daggy (New York: Crossroad, 1989)

LG   *Loretto and Gethsemani* (Trappist, Ky.: Abbey of Gethsemani, 1961)

LL   *Love and Living,* ed. Naomi Burton Stone and Brother Patrick Hart (New York: Farrar, Straus & Giroux, 1979)

MZM   *Mystics and Zen Masters* (New York: Farrar, Straus & Giroux, 1967)

NMII   *No Man Is an Island* (New York: Harcourt Brace, 1955)

NS   *New Seeds of Contemplation* (New York: New Directions, 1962)

PM   *The Poorer Means: A Meditation on Ways to Unity* (Haywards Heath, England: Holy Cross Convent, 1965).

PP   *Passion for Peace: The Social Essays,* ed. William H. Shannon (New York: Crossroad, 1995)

RJ   *The Road to Joy: Letters to New and Old Friends,* ed. Robert E. Daggy (New York: Farrar, Straus & Giroux, 1989)

TMA   *Thomas Merton in Alaska: The Alaskan Conferences, Journals and Letters,* ed. Robert E. Daggy (New York: New Directions, 1989)

WF   *Witness to Freedom: Letters in Times of Crisis,* ed. William H. Shannon (New York: Farrar, Straus & Giroux, 1994)

"A Life Free from Care," *Cistercian Studies* 5 (1970)

Preface to a Collection of Prayers (unpublished manuscript)

Acknowledgments

Grateful acknowledgment is made to the following publishers for permission to reprint from copyrighted material:

The Crossroad Publishing Company for selections from *"Honorable Reader": Reflections on My Work* by Thomas Merton, ed. Robert E. Daggy (New York: Crossroad, 1989) copyright © by The Trustees of the Merton Legacy Trust; *Passion for Peace: The Social Essays* by Thomas Merton, ed. William H. Shannon (New York: Crossroad, 1995) copyright © by The Trustees of the Merton Legacy Trust.

Doubleday, a division of Random House, for selections from *Conjectures of a Guilty Bystander* by Thomas Merton (New York: Doubleday, 1966) copyright © by The Abbey of Gethsemani.

Farrar, Straus & Giroux for selections from *Courage for Truth: Letters to Writers* by Thomas Merton, ed. Christine M. Bochen (New York: Farrar, Straus & Giroux, 1993) copyright © by The Trustees of the Merton Legacy Trust; *Disputed Questions* by Thomas Merton (New York: Farrar, Straus & Cudahy, 1960) copyright © by The Abbey of Our Lady of Gethsemani, copyright renewed by Alan Hanson; *The Hidden Ground of Love: The Letters of Thomas Merton on Religious Experience and Social Concerns* by Thomas Merton, ed. William H. Shannon (New York: Farrar, Straus & Giroux, 1985) copyright © by The Trustees of the Merton Legacy Trust; *Love and Living* by Thomas Merton, ed. Naomi Burton Stone and Brother Patrick Hart (New York: Farrar, Straus & Giroux, 1979) copyright © by The Trustees of the Merton Legacy Trust; *Mystics and Zen Masters* by Thomas Merton (New York: Farrar, Straus & Giroux, 1967) copyright © by The Abbey of Gethsemani, copyright renewed by the Trustees of the Merton Legacy Trust; *The Road to Joy: Letters to New and Old Friends* by Thomas Merton, ed. Robert E. Daggy (New York: Farrar, Straus & Giroux, 1989) copyright © by The Trustees of the Merton Legacy Trust; *Witness to Freedom: Letters in Times of Crisis* by Thomas Merton, ed. William H. Shannon (New York: Farrar, Straus & Giroux, 1994) copyright © by The Trustees of the Merton Legacy Trust.

Thomas Merton's Life and Work:
A Brief Overview

1915	January 31. Born at Prades, France, son of Owen Merton (artist from New Zealand) and Ruth Jenkins (artist from the United States)
1916	Moved to the United States, lived at Douglaston, Long Island (with his mother's family)
1921	His mother dies from cancer
1922	In Bermuda with his father, who went there to paint
1925	In France with his father, lived at St. Antonin
1926	Entered Lycée Ingres, Montauban, France
1928	In England, Ripley Court, then Oakham (1929)
1931	His father dies of a brain tumor
1932	At Oakham acquired a scholarship to Clare College, Cambridge
1933	Visited Italy, spent the summer in the United States, entered Cambridge in the fall; studied modern languages (French and Italian)
1934	Left Cambridge and returned to the United States
1935	Entered Columbia University
1937	At Columbia was the editor of the 1937 yearbook and the art editor of the *Columbia Jester*
1938	Graduated from Columbia, began work on M.A.
	November 16. Received into the Catholic Church at Corpus Christi Church
1940–41	Taught English at St. Bonaventure University

1941   December 10. At age twenty-six entered the Abbey of Our
          Lady of Gethsemani, Trappist, Kentucky

1944   March 19. Simple vows

          Thirty Poems

1946   *A Man in the Divided Sea*

1947   March 19. Solemn vows

1948   Publication of best-seller autobiography, *The Seven Storey
          Mountain*

1949   May 26. Ordained priest

          *Seeds of Contemplation, The Tears of the Blind Lions, The
          Waters of Siloe*

1951–55   Master of Scholastics (students for priesthood)

1951   *The Ascent to Truth*

1953   *The Sign of Jonas*

1955   *No Man Is an Island*

1955–65   Master of Novices

1956   *The Living Bread*

1957   *The Silent Life*

          The Strange Islands

1958   *Thoughts in Solitude*

1959   *The Secular Journal of Thomas Merton*

          Selected Poems

1960   *Disputed Questions*

          The Wisdom of the Desert

1961   *The New Man*

1962   *New Seeds of Contemplation*

1963   *Emblems of a Season of Fury*

1964   *Seeds of Destruction*

1965   *Gandhi on Non-Violence*

           The Way of Chuang Tzu

           Seasons of Celebration

1965–68   Lived as a hermit on the grounds of the monastery

1966   *Raids on the Unspeakable*

           Conjectures of a Guilty Bystander

1967   *Mystics and Zen Masters*

1968   *Monks Pond*

           Cables to the Ace

           Faith and Violence

           Zen and the Birds of Appetite

1968   December 10. Died at Bangkok, Thailand, where he had spoken at a meeting of Asian Benedictines and Cistercians.

POSTHUMOUS PUBLICATIONS

1969   *My Argument with the Gestapo*

           Contemplative Prayer

           The Geography of Lograire

1971   *Contemplation in a World of Action*

1973   *The Asian Journal of Thomas Merton*

1976   *Ishi Means Man*

1977   *The Monastic Journey*

           The Collected Poems of Thomas Merton

1979   *Love and Living*

1980   *The Non-Violent Alternative*

1981   *The Literary Essays of Thomas Merton*

           Day of a Stranger

Preface

In each age, there are people to whom we turn for lessons in how to live more truly and more deeply. They are the guides and gurus, the prophets and saints whose spiritual journeys illumine ours. Although Merton would have eschewed the designation "spiritual master," it is clear that he emerged as a voice to be listened to — even during his own lifetime. The astounding success of *The Seven Storey Mountain* had cast Thomas Merton in the role of a spokesman for the contemplative life. In subsequent books, he drew on his experience as a contemplative and his gifts as a writer to map the terrain of the inner life. He became, in his own words, "an explorer" who felt himself "summoned to explore a desert area of the human heart." Having established himself as a "spiritual writer," he soon expanded the boundaries of his "spiritual writing" as his contemplative practice awakened in him the desire to work for justice and peace. With a sense of urgency, he spoke out against war and against violence. His contemplative spirituality blossomed into a spirituality of compassion.

Merton's spirituality was deeply rooted in the Christian monastic and mystical tradition, so deeply rooted that Merton became increasingly comfortable in moving beyond the boundaries of Christianity. Ever a faithful Catholic, he nevertheless found that he was at home with Anglicans and Baptists, with Jews and Muslims, with Hindus and Buddhists. Deeply grounded in his own tradition, he easily moved beyond cultural and religious boundaries to reach out to and connect with persons whose experiences and perspectives were different from his own, believers and unbelievers alike. In contacts with intellectuals and poets, with writers and activists, and with ordinary people, he witnessed to the possibility of life lived more deeply. His way of life spoke as eloquently as did his writings.

When he died in December 1968, Merton's prominence as a religious figure and writer merited an obituary on the front page of the *New York Times*. The obituary, written by Israel Shenker, identified Merton as "the Trappist monk who spoke from the world of silence to questing millions who sought God." Merton continued to speak out through his writings: books published during his lifetime have been reprinted and reissued, and his posthumous publications are almost as numerous as works published while he was alive. Among recent publications are five volumes of letters and seven volumes of personal journals. In the last few years, Merton has found yet another venue for his work: the Internet. Numerous web sites (including one maintained by the Abbey of Gethsemani) invite readers to learn about his life story, review lists of his writings, peruse articles and papers that explore aspects of his thought, and learn about the monastic way of life. I cannot help wondering what Merton would have made of this, but I am quite certain he would have been pleased to discover a new way to encounter readers. After all, a writer wants nothing more than to be read.

The continued interest in Merton suggests that people want and need to hear what he has to say. Sharing the wisdom of one whose heart awakened to the reality of God within him — a God who calls people to justice and love — Merton touches and moves readers still. He awakens the hearts of readers because he shares the wisdom of an awakened heart.

Selecting texts for this anthology of Merton's writings has been both a pleasure and a challenge. It has been a delight to read and reread Merton and to return to familiar texts, only to experience the surprise of coming across lines I had never *really* read before. And I have enjoyed reading some texts I never *did* read before. But, given the limits of space, I found it difficult to make choices and to omit pieces I would have liked to include. I soon realized that these selections could only offer "a taste of Merton" intended to lure readers to read more of Merton for themselves. This is, I am sure, a goal I share with editors of earlier Merton anthologies.

I wish to mention three anthologies. The first is *The Thomas Merton Reader,* edited by Thomas P. McDonnell (Harcourt Brace, 1962). Merton himself was involved in preparing the *Reader* and even wrote a preface for it, in which he reflected on his work as a writer and a quarter of a century of his writings. Distinguishing between his early efforts and more recent writings, he counted the latter as his "most significant," singling out books such as *Disputed Questions, The Wisdom of the Desert,* and *New Seeds of Contemplation* and essays on war and solitude. McDonnell's anthology remains an impressive and comprehensive selection that demonstrates the range and depth of Merton's writing over time by drawing together a variety of genres and illustrating a variety of themes at play in his work.

More recently two substantial anthologies of Merton's work have been published: *Thomas Merton Spiritual Master: The Essential Writings* (Paulist Press, 1992), edited by Lawrence Cunningham, and *Passion for Peace: The Social Essays* (Crossroad, 1995), edited by William H. Shannon. Each focuses on a dimension of Merton's person and writing: Cunningham focuses "almost entirely" on Merton's "spiritual life," and Shannon on Merton's prophetic witness. Cunningham's selections from Merton's autobiographical and spiritual writings along with his insightful introduction focus the reader's attention on the contemplative dimension of Merton's spirituality. Shannon's selection of essays on war, peace, racism, civil rights, and nonviolence highlights Merton's role as a social critic and prophet. Arranged chronologically, the selections reveal the way in which Merton's passion for peace expressed itself in his writings from 1961 to 1968. Shannon's introduction to the volume and the introductory notes preceding each essay show how Merton's social concerns unfold and fit into his life and work. McDonnell's *Reader* and Cunningham's and Shannon's anthologies deepen our understanding and appreciation of Merton.

I hope this book will do the same. While it does not necessarily represent "the best" of Merton's writings, nor is it a comprehensive collection of his writings, this book brings together a selection of writings that explore three themes that are especially significant to Merton's spirituality: contemplation, compassion, and unity.

I have drawn selections from a variety of sources: some well known, others less so, and some not easily accessed elsewhere. The selections represent a variety of genres — prose and poetry, journals and letters, as well as some transcriptions of talks Merton gave. The latter, though unpolished, capture something of Merton's voice and style as he shared ideas close to his heart.

One additional note: Writing in the forties, fifties, and sixties, Merton observed the linguistic conventions of his day with regard to gender. Readers who have come to expect inclusive language will find Merton's constant reference to "men" and his exclusive use of male pronouns somewhat jarring. I am not the first to observe that were Merton writing today he would employ inclusive language. But alas he was writing then and not now. Merton's texts are reproduced here as he wrote them. I trust that the inclusivity of his message transcends the exclusivity of his language.

Writing to a student who had asked him how to study, Merton advised the young man to study "to find the truth and to awaken deeper levels of life in yourself." May we who read and study Merton do just that.

I am grateful to Robert Ellsberg for the invitation to do this volume and for his counsel and encouragement; to my colleagues at Nazareth College of Rochester, especially Robert Miller, President, Dennis Silva, Vice-President for Academic Affairs, and William H. Shannon, Professor Emeritus, for their continued support; and to Diane Kehrli and Mary Savoie-Leopold for their assistance. I also wish to express my appreciation to the Kilian J. and Caroline F. Schmitt Foundation. Appointment to the Schmitt Endowed Chair, for 1999–2001, has enabled me to complete this project and begin others.

Introduction

Awakening the Heart

✚

Some twenty-five years after they met in Dharamsala, India, in October 1968, the Dalai Lama wrote about Thomas Merton in his autobiography: "More striking than his outward appearance, which was memorable in itself, was the inner life that he manifested. I could see he was a truly humble and deeply spiritual man. This was the first time I had been struck by such a feeling of spirituality in anyone who professed Christianity.... It was Merton who first introduced me to the real meaning of the word 'Christian' " (*Freedom in Exile*, 189). The Dalai Lama was not the only one for whom Merton broke open the meaning of the word "Christian." Having actually met Merton, the Dalai Lama experienced what countless readers have sensed: Merton's spirituality was embodied in his person. It is not only what Merton said or wrote but also who he was that touched people. This is not to discount the truth or power of his writings. It is only to emphasize the integral relationship between Merton's words and Merton's life. Merton himself recognized this: "Every book I write," he confessed in *The Sign of Jonas*, "is a mirror of my own character and conscience" (*The Sign of Jonas*, 165). Looking back on his work some twenty years later, he remained convinced that his best writing was "confession and witness" (*Learning to Love*, 371).

"Confession and witness" aptly characterize the book that made Thomas Merton famous: his best-selling autobiography, entitled *The Seven Storey Mountain*, as well as many of the books that followed. Merton's "confession and witness" revealed what he believed to be essential to living as a Christian and challenged his readers to examine, deepen, and expand their understandings of what living a Christian life entailed. Now more than thirty years after his death, he continues to speak to readers through a body of writings that includes more than a hundred books, countless articles and essays, as well as volumes of published letters and personal journals. Posthumous publications continue to appear in print, as do translations of his writings. Thomas Merton is celebrated as a spiritual master, a prophet, and a man of letters whose life and writing both reflected and helped to shape twentieth-century American Catholicism.

A LIFE IN BRIEF

Thomas Merton was born in France in 1915. Both his New Zealand–born father, Owen Merton, and his American-born mother, Ruth Jenkins, were artists. Both died young: Merton was only six when his mother died and sixteen when he lost his father. By then, Merton had lived in France, the United States, England, and, for a time after his mother's death, in Bermuda. Before he died, Owen Merton appointed Dr. Tom Bennett, his former schoolmate and physician and Tom's godfather, as Tom's guardian. After his father's death, Tom completed his studies at Oakham School and then enrolled at Clare College, Cambridge. Recalling those years in *The Seven Storey Mountain,* Merton acknowledged that Tom Bennett was the person he "most respected and admired and consequently the one who had the greatest influence" on him at that time in his life. "He gave me credit for being more intelligent and mature than I was, and this of course pleased me very much." But Merton added that his godfather would later discover that "his trust in me was misplaced" (*The Seven Storey Mountain,* 78). Merton's raucous and irresponsible behavior at Cambridge led to his being sent back to the United States.

What was intended to be a punishment turned out to be a blessing. Compared to "the dark and sinister atmosphere" of Cambridge, "this big sooty factory [Columbia University] was full of light and fresh air" (*The Seven Storey Mountain*, 137). The radiant light that seemed to surround him at Columbia soon dispelled the inner darkness that overwhelmed Merton at Cambridge. Columbia University's motto — "In Thy light, we shall see light" — put words to the transformation underway in Merton's own heart. He thrived in this newly found light and in the warmth of new friends — among them classmates such as Robert Lax, Ed Rice, Sy Freedgood, and, of course, his teacher Mark van Doren. Merton joined the staff of the *Jester*, contributed to the *Columbia Review*, and became editor of the yearbook. Writing and being with writers was becoming a way of life. In addition to a stream of poems, reviews, and novels, Merton wrote a thesis on William Blake and received a master's degree in English in 1939. Merton would look back at the years he spent at Columbia and the summers he spent with his friends, writing at the Lax family cottage in Olean, New York, as among the best times of his life. "The thing I liked best about Columbia was the sense that the university was on the whole glad to turn me loose in its library, its classrooms, and among its distinguished faculty, and let me make what I liked out of it all. I did" (*Love and Living*, 13).

At Columbia, Merton's reading became "more and more Catholic." In February 1937, he bought a copy of Etienne Gilson's *Spirit of Medieval Philosophy*. Reading Gilson, he discovered "an entirely new concept of God.... What a relief it was for me, now, to discover not only that no idea of ours, let alone any image, could adequately represent God" (*The Seven Storey Mountain*, 174–75). While he was reading William Blake and Aldous Huxley, he was also reading Gerard Manley Hopkins, James Joyce, and Jacques Maritain. In Sep-

tember 1938, Merton was reading G. F. Leahy's life of Gerard
Manley Hopkins.

> All of a sudden something began to stir within me, some-
> thing began to push me, to prompt me. It was a movement
> that spoke like a voice.
>   "What are you waiting for?" it said. "Why are you sit-
> ting here? Why do you still hesitate? You know what you
> ought to do? Why don't you do it?

Urged on by what he had heard, Merton walked nine blocks
to Corpus Christi Church rectory, asked to see Father George
Ford, and announced: "I want to be a Catholic" (*The Seven
Storey Mountain*, 215–16). After almost two months of instruc-
tion from Father Ford, Thomas Merton was received into the
Roman Catholic Church on November 16, 1938. His conversion was only a beginning. The following year as Merton was
planning to begin work on his Ph.D., he realized that he wanted
to be a priest. He began learning about various religious orders, and, encouraged by his friend Dan Walsh, Merton applied
for admission to the Franciscans, who accepted him and then
turned him down. In September 1940, Merton began teaching English at St. Bonaventure University in Olean, New York.
After spending Holy Week of 1941 on retreat at the Abbey of
Gethsemani, Merton decided to become a Trappist monk.

As he was preparing to leave St. Bonaventure's in December
1941, he was certain that he was leaving his old life behind.
He gave away clothes and books and burned the manuscripts
of three and a half novels. He sent a carbon copy of *The Journal of My Escape from the Nazis* (published in 1969, under the
title *My Argument with the Gestapo*) and another journal to
Mark van Doren. Everything else he sent to Lax and Rice. Now,
"with an amazing and joyous sense of lightness" in his heart, he
was ready to go (*The Seven Storey Mountain*, 368). Arriving at
Gethsemani, he spotted the high spire of the monastery church.

I rang the bell at the gate. It let fall a dull, unresonant note inside the empty court. My man got in his car and went away. Nobody came. I could hear somebody moving around inside the Gatehouse. I did not ring again. Presently the window opened, and Brother Matthew looked out between the bars, with his clear eyes and greying beard.

"Hullo, Brother," I said.

He recognized me, glanced at the suitcase and said: "This time have you come to stay?"

"Yes, Brother, if you'll pray for me," I said.

Brother nodded, and raised his head to close the window.

"That's what I've been doing," he said, "praying for you." (*The Seven Storey Mountain*, 371)

For the next twenty-seven years — almost to the day — he lived as a monk of Gethsemani. Merton's initiation to the monastic life followed the usual pattern: novitiate, simple vows, and solemn vows. In *The Sign of Jonas*, Merton notes that Cistercian monks commit themselves to poverty, chastity, obedience, stability, and conversion of manners (*conversio morum* or *conversatio morum*). These sum up "the whole of the monastic vocation." With the vow of conversion of manners, a monk commits himself to continuous conversion of life which involves a life of poverty and chastity. The vow of stability "binds a monk to one monastic community." With this vow, a monk promises fidelity to his community for life, pledging to stay with this community until death (unless he is sent elsewhere by his superiors). "By making a vow of stability the monk renounces the vain hope of wandering off to find a 'perfect monastery'" (*The Sign of Jonas*, 9–10). At different times during his monastic life Merton struggled with stability. Longing for a deeper solitude than appeared possible in the crowded Abbey of Gethsemani during the late forties and early fifties, Merton was

tempted to join the Camaldolese or the Carthusians, with whom
he would be able to live as a hermit in community. But he
resisted the temptation and stayed at Gethsemani, satisfying
himself with the short interludes of silence that were his in the
woods and the hours he spent alone writing in the little shed he
affectionately named St. Anne's. In the late fifties, he explored
the possibility of going elsewhere to live as a monk, this time to
Latin America. When his request for permission to do so was
denied, he appeared relieved.

Following his ordination to the priesthood in 1949, Merton
was, for fifteen years, responsible for the formation of monks:
first as director of scholastics (those preparing for the priesthood) and then as director of novices. During this time, he gave
regularly scheduled conferences in addition to meeting with individuals for spiritual direction. Merton's appointment to these
positions is an indication of how highly he was regarded by
his abbot, Dom James Fox, even though they had their differences, and Merton's long years of service suggest the extent of
his influence on the spiritual formation of the community at
Gethsemani.

In 1965, Merton received permission to live as a hermit on
the grounds of the monastery. Although life in the hermitage
posed its own challenges and the solitude he had longed for was
sometimes a burden, he was grateful at last to have the opportunity to live what, in the last talk he gave to the novices before
moving to the hermitage, he described as "a life free from care,"
a life in which "you cast your care upon the Lord."

Until the last year of his life, Merton rarely left the monastery, except for occasional trips to Louisville for visits to
doctors, hospital stays, and two short trips — one to Col-
legeville, Minnesota, in the company of his abbot Dom James
Fox, and another to New York to meet with Zen Buddhist
writer D. T. Suzuki. In 1968, with the permission of a new abbot, Merton traveled to California, New Mexico, and Alaska,
all the while keeping an eye out for possible sites for a new her-

mitage. He was looking for a remote location where he could live as a hermit without the intrusions that were commonplace at Gethsemani. He felt that the location of his hermitage at Gethsemani made him too accessible to visitors — visitors that the gregarious and sociable monk seemed to enjoy and even encourage. Perhaps, once again, Merton was confronting the challenge of stability.

MONK *AND* WRITER

To understand Merton it is essential to recognize that he was not only a monk but also a writer. His passion for words was evident from an early age. In *Tom's Book,* the "baby book" in which Ruth Jenkins Merton recorded memories of her son's early years, she noted that, by the age of two, he knew five hundred words. Once the talkative child started writing, there would be no stopping him. The young Merton wrote stories and began keeping a journal. In his student years, he found friends who shared his passion for writing, joined the staffs of student publications, and had the pleasure of seeing his work published. He wrote in a variety of genres, producing poems, reviews, and even novels that he submitted, unsuccessfully, to publishers. One of his poems was published in the *New York Times.*

By 1941, Merton's career as a writer appeared to be well underway. But he had presumed that entering the monastery would mark the end of such an occupation. He had even dramatically burned some manuscripts, but he saved some others. His break with the past was not as final is it may have appeared to him to be. Once in the monastery, Merton was surprised to find that not only was he allowed to write, but his superiors were encouraging him to write by assigning him writing work that served the needs of his monastery and his order. In addition to the writing he had to do during the forties, Merton managed

to publish three books of poetry, a history of the Cistercians
(*The Waters of Siloe*), two books on contemplation (*What Is
Contemplation?* and *Seeds of Contemplation*), and a best-selling
autobiography. Merton's prodigious output in his early monastic
years is especially impressive when one realizes how little time
he actually had to write. The daily monastic schedule, with time
dedicated to individual prayer and study as well as to communal
prayer, left very little time for writing. Merton used that time
well. And although he worried a great deal about whether he
could be a monk *and* a writer, he was, in fact, both.

During the fifties, Merton continued to publish poetry as
well as books on monastic and spiritual topics. Some of his
most popular books appeared during this period, including
Thoughts in Solitude, No Man Is an Island, and *The Sign of
Jonas,* a selection of journal entries. Though his censors and
superiors objected that it was unsuitable for a monk to publish such personal material, they relented after Merton's friend,
the French philosopher Jacques Maritain, intervened on Merton's behalf. During the early sixties, Merton again encountered
the resistance of censors and superiors when he began writing
about war and peace. For a time, he was forbidden to publish on the subject because writing about war and peace was
deemed unsuitable for a monk. Merton obeyed the ban, but
when it was lifted he began again to speak out passionately on
social issues, including war, racism, and the abuses of technology. While Merton continued to teach the way of nonviolence,
he wrote about other subjects as well, addressing questions
of belief and unbelief, exploring religions of the East, making
the case for monastic renewal, reflecting on the challenges of
ecumenism and interreligious dialogue, and promoting contemplation within a world of action. Of course, he continued to
write poetry, literary essays, and book reviews, and for a year
he even edited a literary magazine called *Monks Pond.*

In recent years, with the publication of five volumes of
Merton's letters (as well as several books featuring both sides

of Merton's correspondence with individuals such as Czeslaw Milosz, Jay Laughlin, and Rosemary Radford Ruether) and the publication of seven volumes of his personal journals (spanning three decades from 1939 to 1968), readers have learned even more about Merton than he himself revealed in his autobiography or in the selections from his journals published during his lifetime. Merton's letters reveal his ever-widening circle of contacts. Through his letters, he was able to reach beyond the walls of the monastery, beyond rural Kentucky, beyond the United States to connect with people all over the world — among them Boris Pasternak, Jacques Maritain, D. T. Suzuki, and Pablo Antonio Cuadra. Although Merton never met some of his correspondents in person, he came to know many of them "personally." Writing letters became for Merton a way of building and sustaining relationships. He wrote to old friends and family members, to women and men religious, to religious leaders, to social activists, to writers and poets, and to "ordinary people." We learn a great deal about Merton from his letters. Not only do we find out what interested and concerned him; we learn about who he was as a person. In each correspondence, we glimpse something of the man: the sensitive spiritual advisor, the passionate peacemaker, the sharp social critic, the working writer, the true friend, the great enthusiast (and his enthusiasms ranged from the Shakers to the Beat poets to the cultures of indigenous peoples).. Whether he was writing to family or to personal friends, fellow monks, religious or political leaders, writers or poets, philosophers or activists; whether he was responding to inquiries about his work or offering counsel and spiritual direction; whether his correspondents were famous or unknown — Merton took the same care to communicate with each person, and he never repeated himself or gave in to the temptation to recycle a phrase or a line.

While the letters reveal Merton in relationship, his journals allow us to listen in to Merton in conversation with himself.

Merton's journals span a period of thirty years from 1939 to
1968. Reading the journals, we become privy to what was in
his heart from day to day, to what troubled him and to what
made his spirit soar. In his journals Merton expresses his deepest longings and hopes; he vents his frustrations and angers;
he makes plans and records his dreams; he observes the world
around him and explores the world within him; and he prays.
In the journals, we see the many sides of Merton, who could
be pious and iconoclastic, petulant and profound, cerebral and
passionate, insightful and struggling with illusions.

What emerges in Merton's life and through all his writings
is the portrait of a monk *and* writer, a contemplative *and* a
prophet; a person at once simple *and* full of paradox; a man
of conviction *and* no stranger to contradictions; single minded
yet open to new commitments, wanting solitude yet needing in-
timacy, living in silence yet speaking out with passion, deeply
grounded in his own tradition yet open to the wisdom of the
world's religions. Merton emerges as a twentieth-century figure
who, as the Dalai Lama recognized, reveals something of what
it means to be a Christian in our times.

DISCOVERING CHRIST,
BECOMING A CHRISTIAN

Merton discovered Christ, became a Christian, and found out
what it meant to *be* a Christian — in that order. He was eigh-
teen and visiting Rome when he met Christ for the first time.
He found himself "looking into churches" and in the Church of
Sts. Cosmas and Damian, the sight of "a great mosaic, in the
apse, of Christ's coming in judgment in a dark blue sky, with
the suggestions of fire in the small clouds beneath His feet" was
"tremendous" (*The Seven Storey Mountain*, 108). The ancient
churches with their Byzantine museums spoke to him:

And now for the first time in my life I began to find out something of Who this Person was that men called Christ. It was obscure, but it was a true knowledge of Him, in some sense, truer than I knew and truer than I would admit. But it was in Rome that my conception of Christ was formed. It was there I first saw Him, Whom I now serve as my God and my King and Who owns and rules my life. (*The Seven Storey Mountain*, 110)

One night, during his stay in Rome, he experienced a spiritual awakening.

I was in my room. It was night. The light was on. Suddenly it seemed to me that Father, who had been dead more than a year, was there with me. The sense of his presence was as vivid and as real and as startling as if he had touched my arm or spoken to me. The whole thing passed in a flash, but in that flash, instantly, I was overwhelmed with a sudden and profound insight into the misery and corruption of my own soul, and I was pierced deeply with a light that made me realize something of the condition I was in, and I was filled with horror at what I saw, and my whole being rose up in revolt against what was within me, and my soul desired escape and liberation and freedom from all this with an intensity and an urgency unlike anything I had ever known before. And now I think for the first time I really began to pray — praying not with my lips and with my intellect and my imagination, but praying out of the very roots of my life and of my being, and praying to the God I had never known, to reach down towards me out of His darkness and to help me get free of the thousand terrible things that held my will in their slavery. (*The Seven Storey Mountain*, 111)

He felt "as though" his father had actually "communicated" to him "without words an interior light from God" — in which he could see himself as he was. The following day he went to the Church of Santa Sabina to pray. And though self-conscious and afraid he might he thrown out, he prayed. Walking out, he felt as though he had been reborn. The intensity of that moment passed and it would be several years before he again found himself drawn to a church, this time to Corpus Christi, near Columbia, and about five years before he was received into the Catholic Church on November 16, 1938.

Merton was twenty-three when became a Catholic and almost twenty-seven when he entered the monastery. As a monk, Merton continued to learn what it meant to be a Christian in the "school of charity," that is, the monastery, and to share what he had learned through the personal witness of his life and his writing. Three dimensions of Christianity are especially striking in Merton's life and writing: its contemplative dimension, its commitment to social justice and compassion, and its vision of unity. In other words, being a Christian involves awakening to the reality of God within, living with love and justice, and recognizing and sustaining all that unites the human community. Looking at particular times in Merton's life can serve to focus attention on how Merton came to experience and express these dimensions of Christianity. Each serves as an entrée into Merton's life and the development of his thought.

AWAKENING THE
CONTEMPLATIVE WITHIN

On December 28, 1947, Thomas Merton received a telegram from Robert Giroux at Harcourt, Brace. It read: "Manuscript accepted. Happy New Year." His literary agent Naomi Burton (Stone) had sent the manuscript to Giroux only a week before. Neither Robert Giroux nor Naomi Burton, neither Thomas Merton himself nor Abbot Frederic Dunne could have anticipated how well *The Seven Storey Mountain* would be received by readers. However, three well-known authors to whom Bob Giroux had sent the galleys — Evelyn Waugh, Graham Greene, and Clare Boothe Luce — responded with enthusiastic endorsements that suggested how positively readers would respond to *The Seven Storey Mountain*. The *Mountain*, as Merton referred to it, was published on October 4, 1948, and, in May 1949, Bob Giroux presented Merton with the one hundred thousandth copy. Sales of the original cloth edition exceeded six hundred thousand copies.

The publication of *The Seven Storey Mountain* marked the beginning of Thomas Merton's "public story." Book jacket blurbs compared the autobiography to Augustine's *Confessions*. A reviewer in the *New York Herald Tribune* observed, "The fervor of his progress to the Trappist monastery at Gethsemani is deeply moving. It is a difficult matter to write about, but I think there will be many who, however alien the experience may remain to them personally, will put the narrative down with wonder and respect." Another reviewer proclaimed the book "a hymn of faith." Still another announced that it would appeal to Catholic and non-Catholic alike. Fifteen years later, Merton himself acknowledged that *The Seven Storey Mountain,* written when he was "still quite young," had acquired a life of its own. And although the mature Merton found the image created by *The Seven Storey Mountain* — the image of "the official voice of Trappist silence, the monk with his hood up and his back to the camera, brooding over the water of an artificial lake" — out of character with the monk he had become, he acknowledged that *The Seven Storey Mountain* was what it was. "The story no longer belongs to me," Merton observed, in 1963, in his preface to the Japanese edition of *The Seven Storey Mountain.*

> I have no right to tell it in a different way, or to imagine that it should have been seen through wiser eyes. In its present form, which will remain its only form, it belongs

to many people. The author no longer has an exclusive claim upon his story. (*"Honorable Reader,"* 63)

In *The Seven Storey Mountain*, Merton chronicled the spiritual awakening that led him to the Catholic Church and drew him to the monastery of Gethsemani. Though relatively few would follow him into the monastery, many who read his autobiography would resonate with his restlessness, his searching, and his discovery of life's deeper meaning. Merton showed his readers that there was another dimension to life, that life could be lived on a deeper level if one allows oneself to be discovered by God. This is life's contemplative dimension.

Merton concludes the epilogue to his autobiography with a prayer — in the midst of which he hears God speaking to him. He is reminded that God's mercy brought him "from Prades to Bermuda to St. Antonin to Oakham to London to Cambridge to Rome to New York to Columbia to Corpus Christi to St. Bonaventure to the Cistercian Abbey of the poor men who labor in Gethsemani" (*The Seven Storey Mountain*, 423). God was with him in all these places: the place he was born; the places where he lived during his childhood and youth; the places where he went to school; the places where he made friends and enjoyed their company; the places where he experienced the first stirrings of faith; the places where he studied and professed that faith; the places where he first heard, then nurtured, the call to become a monk; and finally the place where he found peace within the "four walls" of his new freedom. Remembering this journey, he recognized that it was God who led him to and through each of these places. Each place had left its imprint upon him but, as he concludes his autobiography, it is not the individual places and what he experienced in each that finally matter. Rather, it is his awareness of the God whom he encountered and finally recognized in each place that mattered most. Merton realized that it was God who brought him from slavery to freedom: the God of mercy and of grace — "God, that center

Who is everywhere, and whose circumference is nowhere, finding me, through incorporation with Christ, incorporated into the immense and tremendous gravitational movement which is love, which is the Holy Spirit, loved me. And He called out to me from His own immense depths" (*The Seven Storey Mountain*, 225).

Later, he put this experience in other words:

> Every moment and every event of every man's life on earth plants something in his soul. For just as the wind carries thousands of winged seeds, so each moment brings with it germs of spiritual vitality that come to rest imperceptibly in the minds and wills of men. Most of these unnumbered seeds perish and are lost, because men are not prepared to receive them: for such seeds as these cannot spring up anywhere except in the good soil of freedom, spontaneity and love. (*New Seeds of Contemplation*, 14)

God had sown many seeds in his own soul, and though some perished, others took root and flourished.

As Merton described the exterior journey that brought him to the Catholic Church and the Abbey of Gethsemani, he revealed something of the inner journey that brought him to God and awakened the contemplative within him. "The geographical pilgrimage," he would later write, "is the symbolic acting out of an interior journey" (*Mystics and Zen Masters*, 92).

The Seven Storey Mountain introduced readers to the contemplative dimension of Christianity, and thereafter contemplation became the cornerstone of Merton's spirituality and the major theme in his writing. It may be helpful to note that Merton used the term "contemplation" in two ways: to name silent *wordless prayer* and to name the actual *experience* of God in prayer. Describing his own way of contemplation, that is, of contemplative prayer, in a letter to his Muslim friend Abdul Aziz, Merton says that it is "a very simple way of prayer . . .

centered entirely on attention to the presence of God." It "does not mean imagining anything or conceiving a precise image of God," but simply adoring God "as invisible and infinitely beyond our comprehension, and realizing Him as all." Merton's way of prayer "is not 'thinking about' anything, but a direct seeking of the Face of the Invisible, which cannot be found unless we become lost in Him who is Invisible" (*The Hidden Ground of Love,* 63–64).

Contemplative prayer, Merton knew, could prepare a person for the experience of God which is the gift of contemplation. As he continued to write about contemplation, Merton found various ways to express what he wanted to say using metaphors like awakening, becoming aware, and being born again. Contemplation is awakening to "a new level of reality" and to "the new life of the self." Contemplation is becoming aware of who I truly am in God. Contemplation is a rebirth. In contemplation, we journey inward and discover our union with God and with one another.

Merton's message is simple: it is possible to experience God, to awaken to and become aware of God's presence. And in doing so, it is possible to become real and whole, to become truly oneself. Although the silence and solitude of the monastery create a space conducive to contemplation, contemplation is not restricted to monks. Contemplation is God's own self-gift; it is freely given, a gift from God that can be received wherever one is. Even in *The Seven Storey Mountain,* in which Merton celebrates the distinctive character of the contemplative life which can be lived to the full in the monastery, he acknowledges that "you [the reader] are called to a deep interior life, perhaps even to mystical prayer, and to pass the fruits of contemplation on to others" (*The Seven Storey Mountain,* 507). In 1967, in one of two letters he wrote in response to a request from Pope Paul VI (via Dom Francis Decroix) to offer input into a message of contemplatives to persons in the world, Merton reiterated the universality of the call to contemplation:

The contemplative life should not be regarded as the exclusive prerogative of those who dwell in monastic walls. All men can seek and find this intimate awareness and awakening which is a gift of love and a vivifying touch of creative and redemptive power, that power which raised Christ from the dead and cleanses us from dead works to serve the living God.... It should certainly be emphasized today that prayer is a real source of personal freedom in the midst of a world in which men are dominated by massive organizations and rigid institutions which seek only to exploit them for money and power. Far from being the cause of alienation, true religion in spirit is a liberating force that helps man to find himself in God. (*The Hidden Ground of Love,* 159)

For twenty years after the success of *The Seven Storey Mountain* had cast him as a spokesman for the contemplative life, Merton was still writing about contemplation, still searching for ways to get across what he saw to be at the core of Christianity, looking for ways to let it be known that God reaches out to us in love and that the "secret" of our identity is "hidden in the love and mercy of God.... If I find Him I will find myself and if I find my true self I will find Him" (*New Seeds of Contemplation,* 35–36). As he wrote about contemplation, Merton found the words to talk about the God who is within us and the discovery of our truest selves in God.

FROM CONTEMPLATION
TO COMPASSION TO PEACE

By the late fifties, Merton had, in a real way, returned to the world that he had left behind when he entered the monastery in 1941. In 1958, in a now well-known experience, Merton had a vision at a street corner in Louisville that symbolized a transformation in his sense of himself, his understanding of his vocation, and his relationship to the world at large. The day after his epiphany at Fourth and Walnut, Merton described the experience in his journal.

> Yesterday, in Louisville, at the corner of 4th and Walnut, suddenly realized that I loved all these people and that none of them were, or could be, totally alien to me. As if waking from a dream — the dream of my separateness, of the "special" vocation to be different. My vocation does not really make me different from the rest of men or put me in a special category except artificially, juridically. I am still a member of the human race — and what more glorious destiny is there for man, since the Word was made flesh and became, too, a member of the Human Race! (*A Search for Solitude*, 181–82)

Later, as he was preparing for publication a book of selections from his journals, Merton elaborated on his initial description of this transforming vision. Awakened from the illusion of a "separate holy existence," Merton recognized his unity with others and his involvement in the world: "though 'out of the world' we are in the same world as everybody else, the world of the bomb, the world of race hatred, the world of technology, the world of mass media, big business, revolution, and all the rest." This sense of being "in the world" was coupled with an insight about the significance of the Incarnation: "I have the immense joy of being *man*, a member of a race in which God Himself became incarnate." All is transformed. At Fourth and Walnut, in the middle of the shopping district, Merton saw others as they *really are:* "the secret beauty of their hearts, the depths of their hearts where neither sin nor desire nor self-knowledge can reach, the core of their reality, the person that each one is in God's eyes." If only they could see themselves and others in this way, there would be "no more war, no more hatred, no more cruelty, no more greed" (*Conjectures of a Guilty By-*

stander, 156–58). In one sense, Merton's vision at Fourth and Walnut was a spontaneous awakening. It was a flash of insight. In another sense, the seeds for the experience had been sown much earlier. His experience in Louisville symbolized a change in his self-understanding that had long been underway as his awareness of God's presence deepened within him.

Merton put words to his new vision of himself, the world, and his place in it in a letter to Pope John XXIII, written in November 1958:

> It seems to me that, as a contemplative, I do not need to lock myself into solitude and lose all contact with the rest of the world; rather this poor world has a right to a place in my solitude. It is not enough for me to think of the apostolic value of prayer and penance; I also have to think in terms of a contemplative grasp of the political, intellectual, artistic and social movements in this world — by which I mean a sympathy for the honest aspirations of so many intellectuals everywhere in the world and the terrible problems they have to face. (*The Hidden Ground of Love,* 482)

He explained to Pope John XXIII that he had begun to exercise "an apostolate of friendship" with "a circle of intellectuals" — artists, writers, publishers, and poets. He even proposed the idea of a monastic foundation "whose purpose would be to exercise a contemplative apostolate of this kind" — perhaps in South America.

During the late fifties and throughout the sixties, Merton corresponded with persons around the globe — Latin America, Europe and the Soviet Union, and Asia. Between August and December 1958 alone, Merton wrote to Boris Pasternak, Jacques Maritain, Pablo Antonio Cuadra, Pope John XXIII, Aldous Huxley, and Czeslaw Milosz and, early in 1959, he initiated a correspondence with D. T. Suzuki. News shared by his correspondents and friends as well as what he learned from his reading helped to make him an informed observer of the world around him. But it was through eyes opened wide by prayer that he saw through the illusions and myths that blinded so many others to the realities around them. In the early sixties, the monk whose popularity as a spiritual writer made his a voice to be listened to turned from writing about religious topics such as contemplation and prayer and began speaking out on social issues with prophetic urgency. Not all were ready or willing to listen.

Fired by a vision of a world in which there would be "no more war, no more hatred, no more cruelty," Merton began to build his case for peace. In the summer of 1961, he published two poems that exposed the atrocity of genocide and war: "Chant to Be Used in Processions around a Site with Furnaces," a poem about Auschwitz, and *Original Child Bomb,* a long poem on the atomic bombing of Hiroshima and Nagasaki. Both were poems in which Merton used the words of documentary sources to expose the deadly truth of events that changed the world. In September, he wrote "A Letter to Pablo Antonio Cuadra concerning Giants" in which he called attention to the dangers posed by the superpowers. In October, he published "The Root of War Is Fear" — chapter 17 of *New Seeds of Contemplation. New Seeds* had been approved by the censors. However, Merton had not submitted to the censors the introductory paragraphs that he had added to chapter 17 before sending the piece to Dorothy Day for publication in the *Catholic Worker.* Merton's message was clear: war was *the* issue facing Christians and all people, the danger was imminent and the need for action urgent. In the months that followed, from October 1961 to October 1962, Merton chose from his correspondence 111 letters which he mimeographed in an edition of the "Cold War Letters." Again and again, he repudiated the myths and illusions that obscured the brutal reality of violence and exposed the contamination of speech: "double-talk, tautology, ambiguous cliché, self-righteous and doctrinaire pomposity, and pseudo-scientific jargon that mask a callousness and moral insensitivity, indeed a basic contempt for man" (*Passion for Peace,* 313).

If, through his writings, Merton became a witness for the way of nonviolence, it was because others had already witnessed to him. Merton was especially influenced by Gandhi's example and teaching.

> In Gandhi's mind, nonviolence was not simply a political tactic which was supremely useful and efficacious in liberating his people from foreign rule, in order that India might then concentrate on realizing its own national identity. On the contrary, the spirit of nonviolence sprang from *an inner realization of spiritual unity in himself.* The whole Gandhian concept of nonviolent action and *satyagraha* is incomprehensible if it is thought to be a means of achieving unity rather than as the fruit of inner unity already achieved. (*Gandhi on Non-Violence,* 6)

Reading Gandhi's writings in the late fifties and early sixties, Merton found himself personally challenged by Gandhi's teaching on nonviolence. When a postulant objected and said Gandhi's nonviolence was "not-natural!" Merton replied, "No, I guess maybe it isn't, and yet without some more of it, what is going to happen to human nature?" (*A Search for Solitude,* 218). Gandhi's witness reminded Merton how he needed "to understand and practice nonviolence in every way" (*Turning toward the World,* 57) and to base his life on truth as Gandhi did. As he gathered texts for *Gandhi on Non-Violence,* Merton thought about how "to transpose" Gandhi's principles to his situation and how "to find a genuinely true and honest position in this world and its belligerent affairs" (*Turning toward the World,* 69).

Gandhi insisted that the roots of nonviolence are to be found within. Merton recognized, as Gandhi had, that the practice of nonviolence required a spiritual transformation, a conversion of the heart. Gandhi himself had found inspiration in the Christian Gospel, and reading Gandhi sent Merton back to his own scriptures. "For the Christian, the basis of nonviolence is the Gospel message of salvation for all. Christian discipleship entails action — loving action which manifests Christ in the world, allowing the Spirit to dwell in and work in us so that we "help to transform others and allow ourselves to be transformed by and with others in Christ" ("Blessed Are the Meek," *Passion for Peace,* 250).

The choice before us, as Merton saw it, is between violence and love. In his preface to the Vietnamese edition of *No Man Is an Island,* Merton put it this way:

> Violence rests on the assumption that the enemy and I are entirely different: the enemy is evil and I am good. The enemy must be destroyed but I must be saved. But love sees things differently. It sees that even the enemy suffers from the same sorrows and limitations that I do. That we both have the same hopes, the same needs, the same aspiration for peaceful and harmonious human life. And that death is the same for both of us. Then love may perhaps show me that my brother is not really my enemy and that war is both his enemy and mine. War is *our* enemy. Then peace becomes possible.

Aware that Vietnamese readers of his book knew firsthand the devastation of war, Merton spoke to them of the "will for reconciliation": "There must be a new force, the power of love, the power of understanding and human compassion, the strength of selflessness and cooperation, and the creative dynamism of the will to live and to build, and the will to forgive" (*"Honorable Reader,"* 124–26).

Merton realized that it is not enough to denounce violence; it is necessary to understand its roots — within the individual and within social structures. The root of war is fear, the fear we have of the other whom we see as the enemy. But the problem of violence is not limited to all-out war.

> The population of the affluent world is nourished on a steady diet of brutal mythology and hallucination, kept at a constant pitch of high tension by a life that is intrinsically violent in that it forces a large part of the population to submit to an existence which is humanly intolerable. . . . The problem of violence, then, is not the problem of a few rioters and rebels, but the problem of a whole structure which is outwardly ordered and respectable, and inwardly ridden by psychopathic obsessions and delusions.

In the face of violence, "a theology of love cannot afford to be sentimental" (*Faith and Violence,* 78–79).

THE UNITY THAT UNIFIES

When Thomas Merton set out for Asia in October 1968, he was embarking on a pilgrimage. For years, he had immersed himself in the texts and teaching of Eastern religions, especially Buddhism. Now he was going to Asia as a pilgrim, "anxious to be able to obtain not just information, not just facts about other monastic traditions but to drink from ancient sources of monastic vision and experience" (*The Asian Journey,* 312–13). Merton had been preparing for this journey, in fact one might say that he had actually been on the journey, for many years. His interest in Eastern religions dates back to his youth as several early "encounters" illustrate. In 1931, when Merton was sixteen and a student at Oakham School, Mahatma Gandhi came to London to represent the Indian National Congress at the Second Indian Round Table Conference. His presence in London and elsewhere in England drew the attention of the press and apparently attracted Merton's attention as well. Merton recalled getting into an argument with the head prefect about Gandhi.

Merton insisted that Gandhi was "right" in "demanding that the British withdraw peacefully and go home," while his opponent questioned how Gandhi could be right "when he was odd." Merton felt the challenge personally: "How could I be right if I was on the side of someone who had the wrong kind of skin, and left altogether too much of it exposed?" (*Nonviolent Alternative*, 178–79). That early "encounter," vividly recalled years later, signaled the beginning of Merton's admiration for the Indian pacifist whose example and teaching helped to shape Merton's own commitment to nonviolence.

Merton was twenty-three and a student at Columbia University when he met Bramachari, a Hindu monk whom Sy Freedgood's wife had befriended in Chicago. Merton paints a vivid picture of their meeting at Grand Central Station: "There stood a shy little man, very happy, with a huge smile, all teeth, in the midst of a brown face. And on the top of his head was a yellow turban with Hindu prayers written all over it in red. And on his feet, sure enough, sneakers" (*The Seven Storey Mountain,* 195). Bramachari came into Merton's life at a time when Merton was fascinated with Oriental mysticism. Reading Aldous Huxley's *Ends and Means* piqued his interest in the subject. But Bramachari seemed to recognize that Merton's interest was more than academic: Bramachari "sensed that I was trying to find my way into a settled religious conviction, and into some kind of a life that was centered, as his was, on God" (*The Seven Storey Mountain,* 195). It was Bramachari who counseled Merton to read "mystical books written by the Christians" such as St. Augustine's *Confessions* and the *Imitation of Christ.* "After all," Merton observed in *The Seven Storey Mountain,* "I had turned spontaneously to the east, in reading about mysticism, as if there were little or nothing in the Christian tradition" (198). Bramachari helped Merton to see otherwise, but Merton never lost his interest in the wisdom of the East.

By the late fifties, Merton was well read in Eastern religious thought and ready for a more substantive interreligious encounter. In March 1959, writing to D. T. Suzuki, Merton called attention to the "Zen quality" of the Desert Fathers and invited Suzuki to write an introduction to *The Wisdom of the Desert*. Suzuki accepted the invitation (*Encounter: Thomas Merton and D. T. Suzuki*, 13). However, Dom Gabriel Sortais, the order's abbot general, refused permission for the inclusion of the introduction in *The Wisdom of the Desert*. Clearly, Merton had been ahead of his time in recognizing the value of an open exchange between a Buddhist and a Catholic priest. Almost a decade later, in the wake of Vatican II, Suzuki's essay finally appeared in *Zen and the Birds of Appetite*.

In 1964, Merton was granted special permission to travel to New York to meet Suzuki in person. Actually meeting Suzuki meant a great deal to Merton: It was "profoundly important to me — to see and experience the fact that there is a deep understanding between myself and this extraordinary and simple man whom I have been reading for about ten years with great attention. A sense of being 'situated' in this world" (*Dancing in the Water of Life*, 116).

Merton's "encounters" were not limited to adherents of Eastern religious traditions. Nor did Merton always initiate the encounters himself. For example, his extensive correspondence with Abdul Aziz, a Muslim living in Pakistan, began with and was driven by Abdul Aziz's many questions about the mysticism in Christianity. It was in the context of their correspondence that Merton both learned about Islam and reflected on all that Muslims and Christians share. It was also in response to Abdul Aziz's inquiry about how he prayed that Merton described his personal way of prayer.

Although Merton was neither a professional ecumenist nor a specialist in interreligious dialogue, his exchanges — in letters and in person — with Hindus, Buddhists, Jews, and Muslims reveal his ability to relate and connect with others on a deep level. Without dismissing the differences between them, he knew that they were meeting on common ground. Merton's letters to D. T.

Suzuki and Abdul Aziz, to Erich Fromm, Abraham Heschel, and Thich Nhat Hanh, among others, demonstrate that Merton lived the truth that he expressed so well in a letter to Amiya Chakravarty and his students at Smith College.

> I do really have the feeling that you have all understood and shared quite perfectly. That you have seen something that I see to be most precious — and most available too. The reality that is present to us and in us: call it Being, call it Atman, call it Pneuma... or Silence. And the simple fact that by being attentive, by learning to listen (or recovering the natural capacity to listen which cannot be learned any more than breathing), we can find ourself engulfed in such happiness that it cannot be explained: the happiness of being at one with everything in that hidden ground of Love for which there can be no explanations. (*The Hidden Ground of Love*, 115)

But it is also important to note that Merton recognized that he stood on common, hidden ground with those for whom religious belief and practice had no meaning. In a particularly candid essay, entitled "Apologies to an Unbeliever," Merton apologized for "the inadequacy and impertinence of so much that has been inflicted... in the name of religion." He described his task as that of "a solitary explorer" who is "bound to search the existential depths of faith in its silences, its ambiguities," where there are "no easy answers" and where "the division between believer and unbeliever ceases to be crystal clear." The problem, as Merton saw it, is not the problem of unbelievers but of believers whose faith has grown cold (*Faith and Violence*, 213).

Nevertheless, Merton was enriched and encouraged by his encounters with those who shared his commitment to the interior life. This is especially well illustrated in Merton's meeting with the Dalai Lama. When Merton met the Dalai Lama in October 1968, their "inner lives" brought them together. Merton viewed his audience with the Dalai Lama as a chance to learn about the meditative practices of Tibetan Buddhism, and the Dalai Lama took the opportunity to learn about Western monasticism. Both monks were deeply knowledgeable about and deeply committed in their traditions. Despite the differences between Buddhism and Christianity, they discovered that they had much in common at the level of practice and experience. Spiritual practices had awakened and nurtured in each a deep inner life. Writing to his friend Ping Ferry, Merton reported: "I had a marvelous eight days in Dharamsala in the Himalayas — three long talks with the Dalai Lama, who is a great guy. All pure gold" (November 11, 1968, *The Hidden Ground of Love,* 244). In a "newsletter" to be circulated among his friends, Merton described the Dalai Lama as "a very alert and energetic person. He is simple and outgoing and spoke with great openness and frankness." Merton reported that they "spoke entirely about the life of meditation, about samadhi (concentration), which is the first stage of the meditative discipline and where one systematically clarifies and recollects his mind." The Dalai Lama insisted "that one could not attain anything in the spiritual life without total dedication, continued effort, experienced guidance, real discipline and the combination of wisdom and methods" (November 9, 1968, *The Road to Joy,* 119), and he had "a lot of questions" about Western monasticism. Reflecting on their meetings in his journal, Merton concluded that they had had "a very warm and cordial discussion" and that they "had become good friends and were somehow quite close to one another." There was "a real spiritual bond" between them (*The Other Side of the Mountain,* 266).

Personal encounters with individuals of other religious traditions — Christian and not — were significant to Merton's story. They served to broaden and to deepen his understanding of religion, both his own religion and that of others. What Merton brought to these encounters was a genuine interest in the other person and his or her religious tradition, coupled with a deep knowledge of and commitment to his own tradition. He was able to see beyond differences to what they shared — to see what united them.

Thomas Merton had a vocation to unity. He had heard the call to unity in the silence of contemplation and he responded with a commitment to peace and justice. He felt himself called to be an instrument of unity. He began by affirming the unity that already is a reality. In his talk to the Temple of Understanding Conference in Calcutta he put it this way: "We are already one. But we imagine that we are not. And what we have to recover is our original unity. What we have to be is what we are" (*The Asian Journey*, 308). These words encapsulate his spiritual vision. Unity is a reality. Unity is our original state. We already are one. But we do not see it and, in our ignorance, live as though we are not one at all. The challenge before us is twofold: to realize the unity that already is and to find ways to live together that are consistent with unity. The unity Merton called for is not a "false unity" based on relativism or syncretism but a "true unity" based on an already existing spiritual bond. His was a contemplative vision of unity.

Unity, as Merton understood it, begins within, and yet the work for unity unifies. "If I do not have unity in myself, how can I even think, let alone speak, of unity among Christians? Yet, of course, in seeking unity for all Christians, I also attain unity within myself." Merton goes on to explain that it is in affirming others that I can realize my own unity: "the more I am able to affirm others, to say 'yes' to them in myself, by discovering them in myself and myself in them, the more real I am. I am fully real if my own heart says *yes to everyone*." Saying "yes" does not mean that one is indifferent to real differences or that one gives in to "the vapid and careless friendliness that accepts everything by thinking nothing." But one "must say 'yes' where one can." He concludes this way: "If I affirm myself as Catholic merely by denying all that is Muslim, Jewish, Protestant, Hindu, Buddhist, etc., in the end I will find that there

is not much left for me to affirm as a Catholic and certainly
no breath of the Spirit with which to affirm it" (*Conjectures
of a Guilty Bystander*, 128–29). This vision represented Merton's growth beyond the parochial perspective that sometimes
comes through in *The Seven Storey Mountain*. During the fifties
and sixties, Merton's Catholicism became more "catholic" as he
discovered the "communion" that is "beyond words...beyond
speech...beyond concept."

Merton modeled a way of ecumenical and interreligious
dialogue that reverenced the person and honored his or her religious tradition. That was his vocation. That was his way. As
he noted in his journal in July 1964,

> Literature, contemplation, solitude, Latin America — Asia,
> Zen, Islam, etc. All these things combine in my life. It
> would be madness for me to attempt to make a "monasti-
> cism" by simply excluding them. I would be less a monk.
> Others have their own way, I have mine. (*Dancing in the
> Water of Life*, 125)

Merton's way of being a Christian and a monk, a mystic and
a prophet, touched the lives of countless people. When he died
in Bangkok on December 10, 1968, his death was noted with
an obituary on the front page of the *New York Times*. Today
more than thirty years later, he continues to speak through his
writings, sharing the wisdom of a spiritual master whose heart
has been awakened.

1

A Call to Contemplation

✠

Our real journey in life is interior: it is matter of growth, deepening, and of an ever greater surrender to the creative action of love and grace in our hearts. —AJ 296

The call to contemplation is at the very core of Merton's spirituality. His writings on contemplation invite persons to experience for themselves the reality of God's presence. For more than two decades, Merton wrote about contemplation—in books and articles, poems and letters—always drawing on his deep knowledge of Christian spirituality and his own ever deepening experience of God. Merton brought attention to a dimension of the Christian life and Christian practice that was unfamiliar to many Christians. He wrote about the "inner experience," about living life fully awake and aware to the reality of God, about being "touched by God," about being born anew. He taught the way of contemplative prayer, a prayer of wordless presence, inviting readers to penetrate below a merely surface existence to live life's Mystery. And though few who read Merton embrace the contemplative life with the intensity possible for monks and hermits, Merton encourages his readers to live more deeply and fully because he has explored and mapped the inner journey for them.

The selections in this chapter dip into an assortment of Merton's writings on contemplation, including his best-known book on contemplation, New Seeds of Contemplation. *Some passages included here are quite well known. Others may be less familiar.*

However, read together, these selections offer a glimpse of what Merton had to say about what contemplation is like; about the necessity of silence, solitude, and prayer; about what it means to discover one's "true self" and to live "free from care." And, as always, Merton's writings invite the reader to go beyond words to experience what words, in their poverty, can never adequately communicate.

AWAKE IN THE DARK

I am out of bed at two-fifteen in the morning, when the night is darkest and most silent....I find myself in the primordial lostness of night, solitude, forest, peace, a mind awake in the dark....A light appears, and in the light an ikon. There is now in the large darkness a small room of radiance with psalms in it. The psalms grow up silently by themselves without effort like plants in this light which is favorable to them. The plants hold themselves up on stems which have a single consistency, that of mercy, or rather great mercy. *Magna misericordia.* In the formlessness of night and silence a word then pronounces itself: Mercy.   —DS 43

THE INTERIOR JOURNEY

In a letter to John Hunt, Thomas Merton proposed to write an article he tentatively entitled "Speaking Out for the Inside." Although he never wrote that article, his proposal stands as an invitation to consider life's "inner dimension." It is an invitation he extended again and again.

Let's see how I can put it in a few words.... An attempt to make people realize that life can have an interior dimension of depth and awareness which is systematically blocked by our habitual way of life, all concentrated on externals. The poverty of a life fragmented and dispersed in "things" and built on a superficial idea of the self and its relation to what is outside and around it. Importance of freedom from the routines and illusions which keep us subject to things, dependent on what is outside us. The need to open up an inner freedom and vision, which is found in relatedness to something in us which we *don't really know*. This is not just the psychological unconscious. It is much more than that. Tillich called it the ground of our being. Traditionally it is called "God," but images and ideas of the deity do not comprehend it. What is it? . . .

The real inner life and freedom of man begin when this inner dimension opens up and man lives in communion with the unknown within him. On the basis of this he can also be in communion with the same unknown in others. . . . Possibly our society will be wrecked because it is completely taken up with externals and has no grasp on this inner dimension of life.

—Letter to John Hunt, December 18, 1966, WF 329–30

•

The way to find the real "world" is not merely to measure and observe what is outside us, but to discover our own inner ground. For that is where the world is, first of all: in my deepest self. . . . This "ground," this "world" where I am mysteriously present at once to my own self and to the freedoms of all other men, is not a visible and determined structure with fixed laws and demands. It is a living and self-creating mystery of which I am myself a part, to which I am myself my own unique door.

—"Contemplation in a World of Action," CWA 170

•

The message of hope the contemplative offers you . . . is . . . that whether you understand or not, God loves you, is present in you, lives in you, dwells in you, calls you, saves you, and offers you an understanding and light which are like nothing you

ever found in books or heard in sermons. The contemplative
has nothing to tell you except to reassure you and say that if
you dare to penetrate your own silence and risk the sharing of
that solitude with the lonely other who seeks God through you,
then you will truly recover the light and the capacity to understand what is beyond words and beyond explanations because
it is too close to be explained: it is the intimate union in the
depths of your own heart, of God's spirit and your own secret
inmost self, so that you and He are in all truth One Spirit.
                              — Letter to Dom Francis Decroix,
                                    August 21, 1967, HGL 158

•

All men can seek and find this intimate awareness and awakening which is a gift of love and a vivifying touch of creative
and redemptive power, that power which raised Christ from the
dead and cleanses us from dead works to serve the living God.
                              — Letter to Dom Francis Decroix,
                                    August 22, 1967, HGL 159

AT LIBERTY TO BE REAL

In this selection from a chapter of New Seeds of Contemplation,
*entitled "Things in Their Identity" Merton observes: "We are at
liberty to be real, or to be unreal. We may be true or false, the
choice is ours." In finding our true selves, we find God or, as
Merton would put it, are found by God.*

A tree gives glory to God by being a tree. For in being what
God means it to be it is obeying Him....
      The more a tree is like itself, the more it is like Him....
      This particular tree will give glory to God by spreading out
its roots in the earth and raising its branches into the air and

the light in a way that no other tree before or after it ever did or will do....

The special clumsy beauty of this particular colt on this April day in this field under these clouds is a holiness consecrated to God by His own creative wisdom and it declares the glory of God.

The pale flowers of the dogwood outside this window are saints. The little yellow flowers that nobody notices on the edge of that road are saints looking up into the face of God.

This leaf has its own texture and its own pattern of veins and its own holy shape, and the bass and trout hiding in the deep pools of the river are canonized by their beauty and their strength.

The lakes hidden among the hills are saints, and the sea too is a saint who praises God without interruption in her majestic dance.

The great, gashed, half-naked mountain is another of God's saints. There is no other like him. He is alone in his own character; nothing else in the world ever did or ever will imitate God in quite the same way. That is his sanctity....

For me to be a saint means to be myself. Therefore the problem of sanctity and salvation is in fact the problem of finding out who I am and of discovering my true self.

Trees and animals have no problem. God makes them what they are without consulting them, and they are perfectly satisfied.

With us it is different. God leaves us free to be whatever we like. We can be ourselves or not, as we please. We are at liberty to be real, or to be unreal. We may be true or false, the choice is ours. We may wear now one mask and now another, and never, if we so desire, appear with our own true face. But we cannot make these choices with impunity. Causes have effects, and if we lie to ourselves and to others, then we cannot expect to find truth and reality whenever we happen to want them. If we have chosen the way of falsity we must not be surprised that truth eludes us when we finally come to need it!

Our vocation is not simply to *be,* but to work together with God in the creation of our own life, our own identity, our own destiny.... We are even called to share with God the work of *creating* the truth of our identity. We can evade this responsibility by playing with masks, and this pleases us because it can appear at times to be a free and creative way of living. It is quite easy, it seems to please everyone. But in the long run the cost and the sorrow come very high. To work out our own identity in God, which the Bible calls "working out our salvation," is a labor that requires sacrifice and anguish, risk and many tears. It demands close attention to reality at every moment, and great fidelity to God as He reveals Himself, obscurely, in the mystery of each new situation. We do not know clearly beforehand what the result of this work will be. The secret of my full identity is hidden in Him....

The seeds that are planted in my liberty at every moment, by God's will, are the seeds of my own identity, my own reality, my own happiness, my own sanctity....

Every one of us is shadowed by an illusory person: a false self.

This is the man that I want myself to be but who cannot exist, because God does not know anything about him. And to be unknown of God is altogether too much privacy.

My false and private self is the one who wants to exist outside the reach of God's will and God's love — outside of reality and outside of life. And such a self cannot help but be an illusion.

We are not very good at recognizing illusions, least of all the ones we cherish about ourselves — the ones we are born with and which feed the roots of sin. For most of the people in the world, there is no greater subjective reality than this false self of theirs, which cannot exist. A life devoted to the cult of this shadow is what is called a life of sin.

All sin starts from the assumption that my false self, the self that exists only in my own egocentric desires, is the fundamental reality of life to which everything else in the universe is ordered. Thus I use up my life in the desire for pleasures and the thirst for experiences, for power, honor, knowledge and love, to clothe this false self and construct its nothingness into something objectively real. And I wind experiences around myself and cover myself with pleasures and glory like bandages in order to make myself perceptible to myself and to the world, as if I were an invisible body that could only become visible when something visible covered its surface....

> The secret of my identity is hidden in the love and mercy of God...
> If I find Him I will find myself and if I find my true self I will find Him....
> The only One Who can teach me to find God is God, Himself, Alone. —NS 29–36

SEEDS OF CONTEMPLATION

God's love seeks our awakening. Contemplation is that awakening.

Every moment and every event of every man's life on earth plants something in his soul. For just as the wind carries thousands of winged seeds, so each moment brings with it germs of spiritual vitality that come to rest imperceptibly in the minds and wills of men. Most of these unnumbered seeds perish and are lost, because men are not prepared to receive them: for such seeds as these cannot spring up anywhere except in the good soil of freedom, spontaneity, and love....

We must learn to realize that the love of God seeks us in every situation, and seeks our good. His inscrutable love seeks our awakening....

For it is God's love that warms me in the sun and God's love that sends the cold rain. It is God's love that feeds me in the bread I eat and God that feeds me also by hunger and fasting.

It is the love of God that sends the winter days when I am cold and sick, and the hot summer when I labor and my clothes are full of sweat: but it is God Who breathes on me with light winds off the river and in the breezes of the wood. His love spreads the shade of the sycamore over my head and sends the water-boy along the edge of the wheat field with a bucket from the spring, while the laborers are resting and the mules stand under the tree.

It is God's love that speaks to me in the birds and streams; but also behind the clamor of the city God speaks to me in His judgments, and all these things are seeds sent to me from His will.

If these seeds would take root in my liberty, and if His will would grow from my freedom, I would become the love that He is, and my harvest would be His glory and my own joy.

—NS 14–17

FULLY AWAKE, FULLY AWARE

[Contemplation is] life itself, fully awake, fully active, fully aware that it is alive. It is spiritual wonder. It is spontaneous awe at the sacredness of life, of being. It is gratitude for life, for awareness, and for being. It is a vivid realization of the fact that life and being in us proceed from an invisible, transcendent, and infinitely abundant Source. Contemplation is, above all, awareness of the reality of that Source. It *knows* the Source, obscurely, inexplicably, but with a certitude that goes both beyond reason and beyond simple faith.... It is a more profound depth of faith, a knowledge too deep to be grasped in images, in words, or even in clear concepts. It can be suggested by words, by symbols, but in the very moment of trying to indicate what it knows the contemplative mind takes back what it has said, and denies what it has affirmed. For in contemplation we know by "unknowing." Or, better, we know *beyond* all knowing or "unknowing."

[Contemplation] knows God by seeming to touch Him. Or rather it knows Him as if it had been invisibly touched by Him. ... Touched by Him Who has no hands, but Who is pure Reality and the source of all that is real! Hence contemplation is a sudden gift of awareness, an awakening to the Real within all that is real. A vivid awareness of infinite Being at the roots of our own limited being. An awareness of our contingent reality as received, as a present from God, as a free gift of love. This is the existential contact of which we speak when we use the metaphor of being "touched by God."

Contemplation is also the response to a call: a call from Him Who has no voice, and yet Who speaks in everything that is, and Who, most of all, speaks in the depths of our own being: for we ourselves are words of his. But we are words that are meant to respond to Him, to answer to Him, to echo Him, and even in some way to contain Him and signify Him. Contemplation is this echo. It is a deep resonance in the inmost center of our spirit in which our very life loses its separate voice and re-sounds with the majesty and the mercy of the Hidden and Living One....

It is awakening, enlightenment, and the amazing intuitive grasp by which love gains certitude of God's creative and dynamic intervention in our daily life. Hence contemplation does not simply "find" a clear idea of God and confine Him within the limits of that idea, and hold Him there as a prisoner to Whom it can always return. On the contrary, contemplation is carried away by Him into His own realm, His own mystery, and His own freedom.   —NS 1–5

•

Contemplation is not and cannot be a function of this external self. There is an irreducible opposition between the deep transcendent self that awakens only in contemplation, and the

superficial, external self which we commonly identify with the
first person singular. We must remember that this superficial "I"
is not our real self. It is our "individuality" and our "empirical
self" but it is not truly the hidden and mysterious person in
whom we subsist before the eyes of God. The "I" that works in
the world, thinks about itself, observes its own reactions, and
talks about itself is not the true "I" that has been united to
God in Christ. It is at best the vesture, the mask, the disguise
of that mysterious and unknown "self" whom most of us never
discover until we are dead. Our external, superficial self is not
eternal, not spiritual. Far from it. This self is doomed to disappear as completely as smoke from a chimney. It is utterly frail
and evanescent. Contemplation is precisely the awareness that
this "I" is really "not I" and the awakening of the unknown
"I" that is beyond observation and reflection and is incapable
of commenting upon itself....

It is not we who choose to awaken ourselves, but God Who
chooses to awaken us.   —NS 7–10

LE POINT VIERGE

Literally le point vierge means "the virgin point." For Merton, it
is a metaphor for the place deep within that is the point of our
encounter with God.

There exists some point at which I can meet God in a real
and experimental contact with His infinite actuality. This is
the "place" of God, His sanctuary — it is the point where my
contingent being depends upon His love. Within myself is a
metaphorical apex of existence at which I am held in being by
my Creator....

This true inner self must be drawn up like a jewel from the
bottom of the sea, rescued from confusion, from indistinction,

from immersion in the common, the nondescript, the trivial, the sordid, the evanescent. . . .

Our discovery of God is, in a way, God's discovery of us. We cannot go to heaven to find Him because we have no way of knowing where heaven is or what it is. He comes down from heaven and finds us. He looks at us from the depths of His own infinite actuality, which is everywhere, and His seeing us gives us a new being and a new mind in which we also discover Him. We only know Him in so far as we are known by Him, and our contemplation of Him is a participation in His contemplation of Himself.

We become contemplatives when God discovers Himself in us.   —NS 37–39

•

At the center of our being is a point of nothingness which is untouched by sin and by illusion, a point of pure truth, a point or spark which belongs entirely to God, which is never at our disposal, from which God disposes of our lives, which is inaccessible to the fantasies of our own mind or the brutalities of our own will. This little point of nothingness and of *absolute poverty* is the pure glory of God in us. It is so to speak His name written in us, as our poverty, as our indigence, as our dependence, as our sonship. It is like a pure diamond, blazing with the invisible light of heaven. It is in everybody, and if we could see it we would see these billions of points of light coming together in the face and blaze of a sun that would make all the darkness and cruelty of life vanish completely. . . . I have no program for this seeing. It is only given. But the gate of heaven is everywhere.   —CGB 158

A NEW BIRTH

Merton's "Preface to the Japanese Edition of The New Man," *written in 1967, begins with the biblical imperative "You must be born again." Merton rewrote the piece in the spring of 1968 and retitled it "Rebirth of the New Man in Christianity." In this excerpt, taken from the revised essay (published in* Cistercian Studies *in 1978 and in* Love and Living *in 1979), being born again is, for Merton, a metaphor for contemplation.*

One of the most important and characteristic themes of Christianity is that of the renewal of the self, the "new creation" of the Christian "in Christ." This death to the "old self" and new life in the Spirit sent by Christ "from the Father" means not only a juridical salvation "in heaven" and "in the hereafter" but much more a new dimension of one's present life, a transformation and renewal not only of the Christian as a person but of the community of believers, the brotherhood of those who have received "the Spirit of Christ" and live in "the grace of Christ."

This renewal of life cannot be understood if it is seen merely as a ritual affair, the result of certain formal, exterior acts.... Nor is it an emotional conversion followed by adherence to a set of new attitudes and convictions, based on this sense of inner liberation....

In the theology of the New Testament, particularly that of Paul and John, the "new being" of the Christian, his "new creation," is the effect of an inner revolution which, in its ultimate and most radical significance, implies complete self-transcendence and transcendence of the norms and attitudes of any given culture, any merely human society. This includes transcendence even of religious practices....

There is in the depths of man's heart a voice which says: "You must be born again." It is the obscure but insistent demand of his own nature to transcend itself in the freedom of a fully integrated, autonomous, personal identity.

When, in St. John's Gospel, Christ says to the Doctor of the Law Nicodemus: "You must be born again," He was not only telling him clearly something that he could hear, if he listened, in the silence and meditation of his own heart. He was also telling him that ordinary answers were not sufficient to meet his demand. To be "born again" is more than a matter of good moral resolutions, of self-discipline, of adjustment to social demands and requirements, of finding oneself a respected and worthwhile role in society. The summons to be "born again" does indeed make itself heard in our hearts, but it does not always have the same meaning, because we are not always capable of interpreting it in its true depth. Sometimes it is little more than an expression of weariness, a sense of failure, an awareness of wrong, a half-hopeless wish that one might get another chance, a fresh start. One desires to begin a new life because the burden of the old has now become an unbearable accumulation of fatigue, mistakes, betrayals, evasions, disappointments. One longs for a new life because the old life is stale, unworthy, uninteresting, cheap. One looks for a new way because all the old familiar ways are a dead end.

Unfortunately, this weariness with the old, this longing for the new, is often just another trap of nature, another variation in the imprisonment we would like to escape. It may inspire us with bright hopes, and it may induce us to believe we have found a new answer: but then, after a while, the same despair regains possession of our heart. Or else we simply fall back into the same old routine. Modern commercial society is built largely on the exploitation of this deep need for "new life" in the heart of man. But by exploiting this need, manipulating and intensifying it, the marketing society also aggravates and corrupts it at the same time. The need for "the new" becomes meretricious and false. It is at the same time insatiable and deceptive. It is tantalized and kept in a state of excitement by all kinds of clever techniques, and it never receives anything but pseudo-satisfactions. Man has more and more needs, more and more hopes, and yet he has become more and more suspicious, less and less able to bear the burden of anxieties and half truths which he carries about in his heart. He feels himself a prisoner in himself, depressed and weighed down by the falsity and illusion of his own life. He knows he needs more desperately than ever to be "a new man" and yet he has lost all real hope of renewal. When he reaches out in desperation for something that promises to renew his jaded existence, he finds himself betrayed again. In the end, he takes to the easier forms of escape. He tries to evade the summons he still hears, however faintly, within his heart....

There is in us an instinct for newness, for renewal, for a liberation of creative power. We seek to awaken in ourselves a force which really changes our lives from within. And yet the same instinct tells us that this change is a recovery of that which is deepest, most original, most personal in ourselves. To be born again is not to become somebody else, *but to become ourselves.*

The deepest spiritual instinct in man is that urge of inner truth which demands that he be faithful to himself: to his deepest and most original potentialities. Yet at the same time, in order to become oneself, one must die. That is to say, in order to become one's true self, the false self must die. In order for the inner self to appear, the outer self must disappear: or at least become secondary, unimportant....

In the Gospel of St. John, we read the conversation in which Jesus speaks of man's new birth....

Nicodemus, the scholar, asks in bewilderment: "How can a grown man be born? Can he go back into his mother's womb and be born again?" This is a natural question of a man who knows life in the world and is suspicious of spiritual and "mystical" delusions. We cannot reverse our course. We cannot really change (he thinks): all we can do is find some better ideal, some discipline, some new set of practices or ideas which will enable us to live the same life with less trouble and fewer mistakes.

But Jesus contradicts this in very forceful language:

Unless a man is born through water and the Spirit
He cannot enter the Kingdom of God.
What is born of flesh is flesh;
What is born of spirit is spirit.
Do not be surprised when I say
You must be born from above.
The wind blows where ever it pleases;
You hear its sound
But you cannot tell where it comes from or where it is
    going.
That is how it is with all who are born of the Spirit.

(John 3:5–8)

In other words, what Jesus speaks of is an entirely new kind
of birth. It is a birth which gives definitive meaning to life. The
first birth, of the body, is a preparation for the second birth,
the spiritual awakening of mind and heart. This is not to be
confused with the awakening of rational consciousness which
makes a human being responsible for his actions as an individual. It is a deep spiritual consciousness which takes man beyond
the level of his individual ego. This deep consciousness, to
which we are initiated by spiritual rebirth, is an awareness that
we are not merely our everyday selves but we are also one with
One who is beyond all human and individual self-limitation.

To be born again is to be born beyond egoism, beyond selfishness, beyond individuality, in Christ. To be born of flesh is to
be born into the human race and to our society, with its fighting, its hatreds, its loves, its passions, its struggle, its appetites.
To be born of the spirit is to be born into God (or the Kingdom of God) beyond hatred, beyond struggle, in peace, love,
joy, self-effacement, service, gentleness, humility, strength. . . .

[The] rebirth of which Christ speaks is not a single event but
a continuous dynamic of inner renewal. Certainly, sacramen-
tal baptism, the "birth by water," can be given only once. But
birth in the Spirit happens many times in a man's life, as he

passes through successive stages of spiritual development.... True Christianity is growth in the life of the Spirit, a deepening of the new life, a continuous rebirth, in which the exterior and superficial life of the ego-self is discarded like an old snake skin and the mysterious, invisible self of the Spirit becomes more present and more active. The true Christian rebirth is a renewed transformation, a "passover" in which man is progressively liberated from selfishness and not only grows in love but in some sense "becomes love." The perfection of the new birth is reached where there is no more selfishness, there is only love. In the language of the mystics, there is no more ego-self, there is only Christ; self no longer acts, only the Spirit acts in pure love. The perfect illumination is, then, the illumination of Love shining by itself. To become completely transparent and allow Love to shine by itself is the maturity of the "New Man."...

"You must be born of the Spirit."

It is not enough to remain the same "self," the same individual ego, with a new set of activities and a new lot of religious practices. One must be born of the Spirit, who is free, and who reaches the inmost depths of the heart by taking that heart to Himself, by making Himself one with our heart, by creating for us, invisibly, a new identity: by being Himself that identity (1 Corinthians 2:6–16; 2 Corinthians 3:12–18; Romans 8:14–17, etc.)....

The Christian civilization of the West has incorporated into itself a great deal of the spiritual dynamism of the Christian faith. "New life" has been interpreted as "new activity" and a more fruitful productive existence.... Christian culture itself has been increasingly dynamic and activistic, and "rebirth" — which remains a central fact of Christian existence — tends to be interpreted in aggressive, activistic, rather than passive, contemplative terms.

The West has lived for thousands of years under the sign of the Titan, Prometheus, the fire stealer, the man of power who defies heaven in order to get what he himself desires. The

West has lived under the sign of will, the love of power, action, and domination. Hence, Western Christianity has often been associated with a spiritual will-to-power and an instinct for organization and authority. This has taken good forms, in devotion to works of education, healing the sick, building schools, order and organization in religion itself. But even the good side of activism has tended toward an overemphasis on will, on action, on conquest, on "getting things done," and this in turn has resulted in a sort of religious restlessness, pragmatism, and the worship of visible results.

There is another essential aspect of Christianity: the interior, the silent, the contemplative, in which hidden wisdom is more important than practical organizational science, and in which love replaces the will to get visible results. The New Man must not be a one-sided and aggressive activist: he must also have depth, he must be able to be silent, to listen to the secret voice of the Spirit. He must renounce his own will to dominate and let the Spirit act secretly in and through him.

— "Rebirth and the New Man in Christianity," LL 192–202

A LIFE FREE FROM CARE

In August 1965, Thomas Merton was granted permission to live full-time in the hermitage. What follows is an excerpt from the last talk he gave to the novices (he had been Master of Novices for ten years) before moving to the hermitage. Reflecting on "freedom from care" as essential for the monk and especially for the hermit, Merton touches on a theme that has relevance for all Christians.

What does the solitary life mean? It is the same as all monastic life. There is one basic, essential thing in the monastic life and in the Christian life, the thing that we all seek in one way or another, and it is some assurance that it is possible in this kind

of life *to put away all care,* to live without care, to not have
to care. Now, what do you mean, "not have to care"? Not to
say: "Well, I don't care. I don't care what they do. I don't care
if they say Mass in Chinese, they won't faze me." No, that's
not it. But the life of the world, in the bad sense of the word,
is a life of care. It is a life of useless care. And it is a life of
self-defeating care, because it is a life which cannot confront
the inevitable fact of death. It is a life which is full of death, it
has death built into it and it cannot get away from that fact.
It circles around and around and it cannot escape the fact that
death is the end of it — and then death comes and death is the
end, period. A life that has nothing but a straight line towards
the grave and a lot of little circular lines to forget the grave as
you travel towards the grave is a life of care, and it is a life of
ever-increasing care and it is a life of frustration and it is a life
of futility. And this is what is meant by the "world" in the bad
sense of the word.

Ideally speaking, the hermit life is supposed to be the life in
which all care is completely put aside. First of all, because it
is a death. It completely accepts death as a completely built-
in fact in life. It is a death to society, it is a death to certain
consolations of society, a death to certain kinds of support,
and it is a renunciation even of care. A person doesn't go into
solitude simply to practice a lot of virtues. If that's what is supposed to happen I'm probably not going to be able to make the
grade. But you go into solitude in order to cast your care upon
the Lord.

Let me read two passages from Caussade which give the
whole essence of it. They are absolutely applicable to the ceno-
bitic life as well as the solitary life. Both are operating on the
same principle. First of all: "Self-abandonment (which is what
we are here for — this business of surrendering totally to God)
is that continual forgetfulness of self which leaves the soul free
to eternally love God, untroubled by those fears, reflections, regrets, and anxieties which the care of one's own perfection and

salvation gives." What he is saying there — of course I should read that through five or six times because each word is important, but we haven't got time — is accusing monks of what we actually do. We come from the world, leaving behind worldly cares, and we come into a little world of the monastery which is full of little cares of its own. The trouble with monastic life, even if it is solitary — in a solitary life you can be devoured by care too — is that it is supposed to be a life without care and we have filled it with care. We are devoured by care — care about our job, care about our life of prayer, care about how we are getting on, care about what other people are doing, care about this, care about that — we're devoured with it. And then the thoughts, "fears, reflections, regrets, and anxieties," this constant business.... Do you deny that our life is a life of care? Do you deny that we are constantly going over, reflecting, reflecting: "He said this, he made this sign and I made this sign, and next time I'm going to make this sign and then he'll drop dead, because it's going to be a real sign — it's going to get across." This is care, you see; these are things we are caring about, and what we are here for is to get rid of that. And of course you get rid of it by going through it.

Here is this beautiful passage, and it's about what I think that I am supposed to do, living up on top of that hill; and this is what I am asking you to pray for, that I may do it, because I think also that it is what you are supposed to do down here and what we are all supposed to do, one way or another: "Since God offers to take upon Himself the care of our affairs, let us once for all abandon them to His infinite wisdom, that we may never more be occupied with aught but Him and His interests." Period. "Since God offers to take upon Himself the care of our affairs . . ." — that is the monastic life and that is above all the solitary life. That is what the solitary life means. It is a life in which you no longer care about anything, because God is taking care of everything. That is why you don't have a great many contacts with the world, you're not terribly occupied with a lot of people and a lot of works and projects: you are simply letting God take care of all those things. All that needs to be taken care of He will take care of (with the help of the interior cellerar, the infirmarian and so forth — they will run up with the band-aid if necessary, but you cast your care upon the Lord).

This is what love is. Let us face the fact for once that what we are here for is love. And what is love? When you love another person you simply forget yourself and think about the other person. You are not concerned with yourself. And if you love this other person and know that it is mutual then you know the other person is thinking about you. So that what happens in love is that each one forgets himself in order to live in and for the other. This is what God asks of us. He asks us to live in such a way that we don't have to think about ourselves, He will think about us....So you are no longer worrying about whether you are virtuous or not, you just live. You live without care and without concern for anything of yourself....

Now what this does — and I know, from what experience I have of it so far, it *does* — is that in fact it is sometimes possible to see that things become transparent. They are no longer opaque and they no longer hide God. This is true. The thing that we have to face is that life is as simple as this. We are living in a world that is absolutely transparent, and God is shining through it all the time. This is not just a fable or a nice story, it is true. And this is something we are not able to see. But if we abandon ourselves to Him and forget ourselves we see it sometimes and we see it maybe frequently: that God manifests Himself everywhere, in everything — in people and in things and in nature and in events and so forth. So that it becomes very obvious that He is everywhere, He is in everything, and we cannot be without Him. You cannot be without God. It's impossible, it's just simply impossible. The only thing is that we don't see it. This again is what we are here for.

What is it that makes the world opaque? It is care. Everything becomes opaque in proportion as we regard it as an individual object and become concerned with it. There is this individual thing, there is this day that I have to live through. It's a particular day and so it's opaque. It comes to me in a big opaque package and I spend my time opening it up. And then when I have taken all the package apart, it's the evening, it's the examination of conscience and I examine myself: and I took all the paper off the package and there *wasn't anything in it*. Then the next day comes along, and that is what we do again. Until a big event comes — I don't know — I get the job of teaching something to the rabbits. It becomes a great thing, and I take the paper off this, piece by piece by piece, and then there's nothing in that either. So you have to leave the rabbits what they are, rabbits; and if you can see that they are rabbits you suddenly see that they are transparent, and that the rabbitness of God is shining through, in all these darn rabbits. And that people are transparent, and that the humanity of God is transparent in people. And that you don't have to take each person as an opaque package: "Who is the mystery of this crazy person here that I have to analyze?" and I look across the choir: "What makes that guy tick?" You don't have to know what makes the man tick. All you have to see is that he is a manifestation of the humanity of God. There is humaneness, humanness, *manness* in God, which is manifested by every human being: not only by the fact that he is a creature of God but by the fact that he is redeemed in Christ. This again is our life, and this is what it is for....

The announcement is the great joy that the Lord is present and living in the world: that the Lord is with us. *Dominus vobiscum,* the Lord be with you. This is what we are constantly announcing in the liturgy, that the Lord is present in the world. It is His world and it belongs to Him and He has manifested its triumph and He is going to make it absolutely clear. And we are not just tending towards a life of abstract immortality because we are spiritual beings with a soul, we are tending towards the full manifestation of the Kingdom of God. And so the disciples at Emmaus — their vocation is our vocation — came running back to Jerusalem bubbling over with joy and happiness not because they understood the mysteries of another world but because they had seen the Lord. This is what we are all here for. We are all here to see the Lord, and to see with the eyes of faith. But to see that the Lord really lives and that the Lord really is the Lord.   — "A Life Free from Care"

SILENCE AND SOLITUDE

Merton wrote "Creative Silence" in April 1968 for the Bloomin' Newman, *published by students at the University of Louisville. He challenges his readers to discover the power of silence.*

Imagine a man or a group of people who, alone or together in a quiet place where no radio, no background music can be heard, simply sit for an hour or a half hour in silence. They do not speak. They do not pray aloud. They do not have books or papers in their hands. They are not reading or writing. They are not busy with anything. They simply enter into themselves, not in order to think in an analytical way, not in order to examine, organize, plan, but simply in order to *be.* They want to get themselves together in silence. They want to synthesize, to integrate themselves, to rediscover themselves in a unity of thought, will, understanding, and love that goes beyond words, beyond analysis, even beyond conscious thought. They want to pray not with their lips but with their silent hearts and, beyond that, with the very ground of their being.

What would prompt modern people to do such a thing?

Are they moved by a sense of human need for silence, for reflection, for inner seeking? Do they want to get away from the noise and tension of modern life, at least for a little while, in order to relax their minds and wills and seek a blessed healing sense of inner unity, reconciliation, integration?

These are certainly good enough motives. But for a Christian there are even deeper motives than this. A Christian can realize himself called by God to periods of silence, reflection, meditation, and "listening." We are perhaps too talkative, too activistic, in our conception of the Christian life. Our service of God and of the Church does not consist only in talking and doing. It can also consist in periods of silence, listening, waiting. Perhaps it is very important, in our era of violence and unrest, to rediscover meditation, silent inner unitive prayer, and creative Christian silence.

Silence has many dimensions. It can be a regression and an escape, a loss of self, or it can be presence, awareness, unification, self-discovery. Negative silence blurs and confuses our identity, and we lapse into daydreams or diffuse anxieties. Positive silence pulls us together and makes us realize who we are, who we might be, and the distance between these two. Hence, positive silence implies a disciplined choice, and what Paul Tillich called the "courage to *be.*" In the long run, the discipline of creative silence demands a certain kind of faith. For when we come face to face with ourselves in the lonely ground of our own being, we confront many questions about the value of our existence, the reality of our commitments, the authenticity of our everyday lives.

When we are constantly in movement, always busy meeting the demands of our social role, passively carried along on the stream of talk in which people mill around from morning to night, we are perhaps able to escape from our deeper self and from the questions it poses. We can be more or less content with the external identity, the social self, which is produced by our interaction with others in the wheeling and dealing of everyday life. But no matter how honest and open we may be in our relations with others, this social self implies a necessary element of artifice. It is always to some extent a mask. It has to be. Even the American taste for frankness, homely simplicity, affability, plainness, and humor is often a front. Some people are naturally that way. Others educate themselves to play this part in order to be accepted by society. Nor is it entirely pretense: it *appeals* to us. But do we ever give ourselves a chance to realize that this talkative, smiling, perhaps rough-and-ready personage that we seem to be is not necessarily our real self? Do we ever give ourselves a chance to recognize something deeper? Can we face the fact that we are perhaps *not interested* in all this talk and business? When we are quiet, not just for a few minutes, but for an hour or several hours, we may become uneasily aware of the presence within us of a disturbing stranger, the self that is both "I" and someone else. The self that is not entirely welcome in his own house because he is so different from the everyday character that we have constructed out of our dealings with others — and our infidelities in ourselves.

There is a silent self within us whose presence is disturbing precisely because it is so silent: it *can't* be spoken. It has to remain silent. To articulate it, to verbalize it, is to tamper with it, and in some ways to destroy it.

Now let us frankly face the fact that our culture is one which is geared in many ways to help us evade any need to face this inner, silent self. We live in a state of constant semiattention to the sound of voices, music, traffic, or the generalized noise of what goes on around us all the time. This keeps us immersed in a flood of racket and words, a diffuse medium in which our consciousness is half diluted: we are not quite "thinking," not entirely responding, but we are more or less there. We are not fully *present* and not entirely absent; not fully withdrawn, yet not completely available. It cannot be said that we are really participating in anything and we may, in fact, be half conscious of our alienation and resentment. Yet we derive a certain comfort from the vague sense that we are "part of" something — although we are not quite able to define what that something is — and probably wouldn't want to define it even if we could. We just float along in the general noise. Resigned and indifferent, we share semiconsciously in the mindless mind of Muzak and radio commercials which passes for "reality."

Of course this is not enough to keep us completely forgetful of the other unwelcome self that remains so largely unconscious. The disquieting presence of our deep self keeps forcing its way almost to the surface of awareness. To exorcise this presence we need a more definite stimulation, a distraction, a drink, a drug, a gimmick, a game, a routine of acting out our sense of alienation and trouble. Then it goes away for the time being and we forget who we are.

All of this can be described as "noise," as commotion and jamming which drown out the deep, secret, and insistent demands of the inner self.

With this inner self we have to come to terms *in silence*. That is the reason for choosing silence. In silence we face and admit the gap between the depths of our being, which we consistently ignore, and the surface which is untrue to our own reality. We recognize the need to be at home with ourselves in order that we may go out to meet others, not just with a mask of affability, but with real commitment and authentic love.

If we are afraid of being alone, afraid of silence, it is perhaps because of our secret despair of inner reconciliation. If we have no hope of being at peace with ourselves in our own personal loneliness and silence, we will never be able to face ourselves at all: we will keep running and never stop. And this flight from the self is, as the Swiss philosopher Max Picard pointed out, a "flight from God." After all, it is in the depths of conscience that God speaks, and if we refuse to open up inside and look into those depths, we also refuse to confront the invisible God who is present within us. This refusal is a partial admission that we do not want God to be God any more than we want ourselves to be our true selves.

Just as we have a superficial, external mask which we put together with words and actions that do not fully represent all that is in us, so even believers deal with a God who is made up of words, feelings, reassuring slogans, and this is less the God of faith than the product of religious and social routine. Such a "God" can become a substitute for the truth of the invisible God of faith, and though this comforting image may seem real to us, he is really a kind of idol. His chief function is to protect us against a deep encounter with our true inner self and with the true God.

Silence is therefore important even in the life of faith and in our deepest encounter with God. We cannot always be talking, praying in words, cajoling, reasoning, or keeping up a kind of devout background music. Much of our well-meant interior religious dialogue is, in fact, a smoke screen and an evasion. Much of it is simply self-reassurance and in the end it is little better than a form of self-justification. Instead of really meeting God in the nakedness of faith in which our inmost being is laid bare before him, we act out an inner ritual that has no function but to allay anxiety.

The purest faith has to be tested by silence in which we listen for the unexpected, in which we are open to what we do not yet know, and in which we slowly and gradually prepare for the day when we will reach out to a new level of being with God. True hope is tested by silence in which we have to wait on the Lord in the obedience of unquestioning faith. Isaiah records the word of Yahweh to his rebellious people, who were always abandoning him in order to enter into worthless political and military alliances. "Your safety lies in ceasing to make leagues, your strength is in quiet faith" (Isaiah 20:15), or as another translation has it, "Your salvation lies in conversion and tranquility, your strength in complete trust." Older texts say "in *silence and hope* shall your strength be." The idea is that faith demands the silencing of questionable deals and strategies. Faith demands the integrity of inner trust which produces wholeness, unity, peace, genuine security. Here we see the creative power and fruitfulness of silence. Not only does silence give us a chance to understand ourselves better, to get a truer and more balanced perspective on our own lives in relation to the lives of others: silence makes us whole if we let it. Silence helps draw together the scattered and dissipated energies of a fragmented existence. It helps us to concentrate on a purpose that really corresponds not only to the deeper needs of our own being but also to God's intentions for us.

This is a really important point. When we live superficially, when we are always outside ourselves, never quite "with" ourselves, always divided and pulled in many directions by conflicting plans and projects, we find ourselves doing many things that we do not really want to do, saying things we do not really mean, needing things we do not really need, exhausting ourselves for what we secretly realize to be worthless and without meaning in our lives: "Why spend your money on what is not food and your earnings on what never satisfies?" (Isaiah 55:2).

— "Creative Silence," LL 38–43

•

Merton's essay "Love and Solitude" is a revision of his 1966 "Preface to the Japanese Edition of Thoughts in Solitude." *In his "Author's Note" Merton proposes that the purpose of the essay is "simply to let solitude speak a little and say something for itself."*

Where is silence? Where is solitude? Where is Love?

Ultimately, these cannot be found anywhere except in the ground of our own being. There, in the silent depths, there is no more distinction between the I and the Not-I. There is perfect peace, because we are grounded in infinite creative and redemptive Love. There we encounter God, whom no eye can see, and in Whom, as St. Paul says, "we live and move and have our being" (Acts 17:28). In Him, too, we find solitude, as St. John of the Cross said, we find that the All and the Nothing encounter one another and are the Same.

If there is no silence beyond and within the many words of doctrine, there is no religion, only a religious ideology. For religion goes beyond words and actions, and attains to the ultimate truth only in silence and Love. Where this silence is lacking, where there are only the "many words" and not the One Word, then there is much bustle and activity but no peace, no deep thought, no understanding, no inner quiet. Where there is no peace, there is no light and no Love. The mind that is hyperactive seems to itself to be awake and productive, but it is dreaming, driven by fantasy and doubt. Only in silence and solitude, in the quiet of worship, the reverent peace of prayer, the adoration in which the entire ego-self silences and abases itself in the presence of the Invisible God to receive His one Word of Love; only in these "activities" which are "non-actions" does the spirit truly wake from the dream of multifarious, confused, and agitated existence.

Precisely because of this, modern Western man is afraid of solitude. He is unable to be alone, to be silent. He is communicating his spiritual and mental sickness to men of the East. Asia is gravely tempted by the violence and activism of the West, and is gradually losing hold of its traditional respect for silent wisdom. Therefore, it is all the more necessary, at this time, to rediscover the climate of solitude and of silence: not that everyone can go apart and live alone. But in moments of silence, of meditation, of enlightenment and peace, one learns to be silent and alone everywhere. One learns to live in the atmosphere of solitude even in the midst of crowds. Not "divided," but one with all in God's Love. For one learns to be a Hearer who is No-Hearer, and one learns to forget all words and listen only to the One Word which seems to be No-Word. One opens the inner door of his heart to the infinite silences of the Spirit, out of whose abysses love wells up without fail and gives itself to all. In His silence, the meaning of every sound is finally clear. Only in His silence can the truth of words be distinguished, not in their separateness, but in their pointing to the central unity of Love. All words, then, say one thing only: that *all is Love....*

Is it true to say that one goes into solitude to "get at the root of existence"? It would be better simply to say that in solitude one *is* at the root....

Solitude is not withdrawal from ordinary life. It is not apart from, above, "better than" ordinary life; on the contrary, solitude is the very ground of ordinary life. It is the very ground of that simple, unpretentious, fully human activity by which we quietly earn our daily living and share our experiences with a few intimate friends. But we must learn to know and accept this ground of our being. To most people, though it is always there, it is unthinkable and unknown. Consequently, their life has no center and no foundation. It is dispersed in a pretense of "togetherness" in which there is no real meaning. Only when our activity proceeds out of the ground in which we have consented to be dissolved does it have the divine fruitfulness of love and grace. Only then does it really reach others in true communion. Often our need for others is not love at all but only the need to be sustained in our illusions, even as we sustain others in theirs. But when we have renounced these illusions, then we can certainly go out to others in true compassion. It is in solitude that illusions finally dissolve. But one must work hard to see that they do not reshape themselves in some worse form, peopling our solitude with devils disguised as angels of light. Love, simplicity, and compassion protect us against this. He who is truly alone finds in himself the heart of compassion with which to love not only this man or that but all men. He sees them all in the One who is the Word of God, the perfect manifestation of God's Love, Jesus Christ.

— "Love and Solitude," LL 20–24

•

"Song: If You Seek... " is included in Merton's Emblems of a Season of Fury, *published in 1963.*

SONG: IF YOU SEEK...

If you seek a heavenly light
I, Solitude, am your professor!

I go before you into emptiness,
Raise strange suns for your new mornings,
Opening the windows
Of your innermost apartment.

When I, loneliness, give my special signal
Follow my silence, follow where I beckon!
Fear not, little beast, little spirit
(Thou word and animal)
I, Solitude, am angel
And have prayed in your name.

Look at the empty, wealthy night
The pilgrim moon!
I am the appointed hour,
The "now" that cuts
Time like a blade.

I am the unexpected flash
Beyond "yes," beyond "no,"
The forerunner of the Word of God.

Follow my ways and I will lead you
To golden-haired suns,
Logos and music, blameless joys,
Innocent of questions
And beyond answers:

For I, Solitude, am thine own self:
I, Nothingness, am thy All.
I, Silence, am thy Amen!

                              —CP 340–41

Without solitude of some sort there is and can be no maturity. Unless one becomes empty and alone, he cannot give himself in love because he does not possess the deep self which is the only gift worthy of love. And this deep self, we immediately add, cannot be *possessed.* My deep self is not "something" which I acquire, or to which I "attain" after a long struggle. It is not mine, and cannot become mine. It is no "thing" — no object. It is "I."

The shallow "I" of individualism can be possessed, developed, cultivated, pandered to, satisfied: it is the center of all our strivings for gain and for satisfaction, whether material or spiritual. But the deep "I" of the spirit, of solitude and of love, cannot be "had," possessed, developed, perfected. It can only *be,* and *act* according to deep inner laws which are not of man's contriving, but which come from God. They are the Laws of the Spirit, who, like the wind, blows where He wills. This inner "I," who is always alone, is always universal: for in this inmost "I" my own solitude meets the solitude of every other man and the solitude of God. Hence it is beyond division, beyond limitation, beyond selfish affirmation. It is only this inmost and solitary "I" that truly loves with the love and the spirit of Christ. This "I" is Christ Himself, living in us: and we, in Him, living in the Father.
  — "Notes for a Philosophy of Solitude," DQ 206–7

A SIMPLE WAY OF PRAYER

Merton describes his own way of prayer in a letter to Abdul Aziz, a Sufi scholar living in Pakistan. Aziz had asked him how he prayed and Merton responded in this way.

Now you ask about my method of meditation. Strictly speaking I have a very simple way of prayer. It is centered entirely on attention to the presence of God and to His will and His love. That is to say that it is centered on *faith* by which alone we can know the presence of God. One might say this gives my meditation the character described by the Prophet as "being before God as if you saw Him." Yet it does not mean imagining anything or conceiving a precise image of God, for to my mind this would be a kind of idolatry. On the contrary, it is a matter of adoring Him as invisible and infinitely beyond our comprehension, and realizing Him as all. My prayer tends very much toward what you call *fana*. There is in my heart this great thirst to recognize totally the nothingness of all that is not God. My prayer is then a kind of praise rising up out of the center of Nothing and Silence. If I am still present "myself" this I recognize as an obstacle about which I can do nothing unless He Himself removes the obstacle. If He wills He can then make the Nothingness into a total clarity. If He does not will, then the Nothingness seems to itself to be an object and remains an obstacle. Such is my ordinary way of prayer, or meditation. It is not "thinking about" anything, but a direct seeking of the Face of the Invisible, which cannot be found unless we become lost in Him who is Invisible.

—Letter to Abdul Aziz, January 2, 1966, HGL 63–64

•

Prayer is not only the "lifting up of the mind and heart to God," but it is also the response to God within us, the discovery of God within us; it leads ultimately to the discovery and fulfillment of our own true being in God.

—Preface to a Collection of Prayers, 1961

•

There are so many words that one cannot get to God as long as He is thought to be on the other side of the words.... That is where the silence of the woods comes in. Not that there is something to be thought and discovered in the woods, but only that the trees are all sufficient exclamations of silence, and one works there, cutting wood, clearing ground, cutting grass, cooking soup, drinking fruit juice, sweating, washing, making fire, smelling smoke, sweeping etc. This is religion. The further one gets ways from this, the more one sinks in the mud of words and gestures. The flies gather.

— Letter to Ludovico Silva, April 10, 1965, CT 225

•

About prayer: have you a garden or somewhere that you can walk in, by yourself? Take half an hour, or fifteen minutes a day and just walk up and down among the flower beds.... Do not try to think about anything in particular and when thoughts about work, etc. come to you, do not try to push them out by main force, but see if you can't drop them just by relaxing your mind. Do this because you "are praying" and because our Lord is with you. But if thoughts about work will not go away, accept them idly and without too much eagerness with intention of letting our Lord reveal His will to you through these thoughts....

— Letter to Sr. Therese Lentfoehr, August 29, 1949, RJ 195

•

[Prayer] means contact with the deepest reality of life, our own truth in [God].... Prayer is the truest guarantee of personal freedom.... We are most truly free in the free encounter of our hearts with God in His word and in receiving His Spirit which is the Spirit of sonship, truth, and freedom. The Truth that makes us free is not merely a matter of information about God but the presence in us of a divine person by love and grace, bringing us into the intimate personal life of God as His Sons by adoption. This is the basis of all prayer and all prayer should be oriented to this mystery of sonship in which the Spirit in us recognizes the Father. The cry of the Spirit in us ... is the heart of our prayer and the great motive of prayer. Hence recollection is not the exclusion of material things but attentiveness to the

Spirit in our inmost heart.... Prayer is a real source of personal freedom in the midst of a world in which men are dominated by massive organizations and rigid institutions which seek only to exploit them for money and power.

— Letter to Dom Francis Decroix,
August 22, 1967, HGL 159

•

Contemplation is really simple openness to God at every moment, and deep peace. And when you say "experience the mysteries of Christ," it just means a deep realization in the very depths of our being that God has chosen and loved us from all eternity, that we really are His children and we really are loved by Him, that there really is a personal bond and He really is present. This is so simple that there is no need to make a commotion about it....

I want to make it quite clear that the whole essence of contemplative prayer is that the division between subject and object disappears. You do not look at God as an object and you don't look at yourself; you are just not interested in yourself. That is the real point.   — TMA 143–44

CONTEMPLATION IN A WORLD OF ACTION

Contemplation is not only for monks. Contemplation has a place in "a world of action."

What does the contemplative life or the life of prayer, solitude, silence, meditation, mean to man in the atomic age? What can it mean? Has it lost all meaning whatever?

When I speak of the contemplative life I do not mean the institutional cloistered life, the organized life of prayer.... I am talking about a special dimension of inner discipline and experience, a certain integrity and fullness of personal development, which are not compatible with a purely external, alienated, busy-busy existence. This does not mean that they are incompatible with action, with creative work, with dedicated love. On the contrary, these all go together. A certain depth of disciplined experience is a necessary ground for fruitful action....

The real point of the contemplative life has always been a deepening of faith and of the personal dimensions of liberty and apprehension to the point where our direct union with God is realized and "experienced." We awaken not only to a realization of the immensity and majesty of God "out there" as King and Ruler of the universe (which He is) but also a more intimate and more wonderful perception of Him as directly and personally present in our own being.... If we are involved only in our surface existence, in externals, and in the trivial concerns of our ego, we are untrue to Him and to ourselves. To reach a true awareness of Him as well as ourselves, we have to renounce our selfish and limited self and enter into a whole new kind of existence, discovering an inner center of motivation and love which makes us see ourselves and everything else in an entirely new light. Call it faith, call it (at a more advanced stage) contemplative illumination, call it the sense of God or even mystical union: all these are different aspects and levels of the same kind of realization: the awakening to a new awareness of ourselves in Christ, created in Him, redeemed by Him, to be transformed and glorified in and with Him. In Blake's words, the "doors of perception" are opened and all life takes on a completely new meaning: the real sense of our own existence, which is normally veiled and distorted by the routine distractions of an alienated life, is now revealed in a central intuition....

Though this inner "vision" is a gift and is not directly produced by technique, still a certain discipline is necessary to prepare us for it. Meditation is one of the more important characteristic forms of this discipline. Prayer is another. Prayer in the context of this inner awareness of God's direct presence becomes not so much a matter of cause and effect as a celebration of love. In the light of this celebration, what matters most is love itself, thankfulness, assent to the unbounded and overflowing goodness of love which comes from God and reveals Him in His world.

This inner awareness, this experience of love as an immediate and dynamic presence, tends to alter our perspective. We see the prayer of petition a little differently. Celebration and praise, loving attention to the presence of God, become more important than "asking for" things and "getting" things. This is because we realize that in Him and with Him all good is present to us and to mankind: if we seek first the Kingdom of Heaven, all the rest comes along with it. Hence we worry a great deal less about the details of our daily needs, and we trust God to take care of our problems even if we do not ask Him insistently at every minute to do so. The same applies to the problems of the world. But on the other hand, this inner awareness and openness makes us especially sensitive to urgent needs of the time, and grace can sometimes move us to pray for certain special needs....

Real Christian living is stunted and frustrated if it remains content with the bare externals of worship, with "saying prayers" and "going to church," with fulfilling one's external duties and merely being respectable. The real purpose of prayer (in the fully personal sense as well as in the Christian assembly) is the deepening of personal realization in love, the awareness of God (even if sometimes this awareness may amount to a negative factor, a seeming "absence"). The real purpose of meditation — or at least that which recommends itself as most relevant for modern man — is the exploration and discovery of new dimensions in freedom, illumination, and love, in deepening our awareness of our life in Christ.

What is the relation of this to action? Simply this. He who attempts to act and do things for others or for the world, without deepening his own self-understanding, freedom, integrity, and capacity to love, will not have anything to give others. He will communicate to them nothing but the contagion of his own obsessions, his aggressiveness, his ego-centered ambitions, his delusions about ends and means, his doctrinaire prejudices and ideas. There is nothing more tragic in the modern world than the misuse of power and action to which men are driven by their own Faustian misunderstandings and misapprehensions. We have more power at our disposal today than we have ever had, and yet we are more alienated and estranged from the inner ground of meaning and of love than we have ever been. The result of this is evident. We are living through the greatest crisis in the history of man; and this crisis is centered precisely in the country that has made a fetish out of action and has lost (or perhaps never had) the sense of contemplation. Far from being irrelevant, prayer, meditation, and contemplation are of the utmost importance in America today. Unfortunately, it must be admitted that the official contemplative life as it is lived in our monasteries needs a great deal of rethinking, because it is still too closely identified with patterns of thought that were accepted five hundred years ago, but which are completely strange to modern man.

But prayer and meditation have an important part to play in opening up new ways and new horizons. If our prayer is the expression of a deep and grace-inspired desire for newness of life — and not the mere blind attachment to what has always been familiar and "safe" — God will act in us and through us to renew the Church by preparing, in prayer, what we cannot yet imagine or understand. In this way our prayer and faith today will be oriented toward the future which we ourselves may never see fully realized on earth.

— "Contemplation in a World of Action," CWA 172–79

LIVING CONTEMPLATIVELY

The contemplative life must provide an area, a space of liberty, of silence, in which possibilities are allowed to surface and new choices — beyond routine choice — become manifest. It should create a new experience of time, not as stopgap, stillness, but as *"temps vierge"* — not a blank to be filled or an untouched space to be conquered and violated, but a space which can enjoy its own potentialities and hopes — and its own presence to itself. One's *own* time. But not dominated by one's own ego and its demands. Hence open to others — *compassionate* time, rooted in the sense of common illusion and in criticism of it. — AJ 117

•

Mercy is the thing, the deepest thing that has been revealed to us by God. A mercy that cannot fail.

It is precisely here we come close to a kind of center of Christian experience, a center from which we can understand everything else. This is the center to which everything else must go just like the spokes go to the center of a wheel. If we do not keep the center in mind and if we do not live in this center, everything then becomes a rat race.

What leads you into this center is a life of prayer. At this center you will experience the love and mercy of God for yourself and find your true identity as a person to whom God has been merciful and continues to be merciful.

What leads up to this discovery is self-knowledge. I must find myself. I must solve my identity crisis, if I have one, then find myself as one loved by God, as chosen by God, and visited and overshadowed by God's mercy...

— "Prayer and the Priestly Tradition," TMA 160–61

2

A Call to Compassion

✚

> Hate is the seed of death in my own heart,
> while it seeks the death of the other.
> Love is the seed of life in my own heart
> when it seeks the good of the other.
>
> —HR 123

Merton's own journey inward returned him to the world he thought he had left behind when he entered the monastery. By the late fifties, he had come to the realization that "the world" had a place in his solitude. As a "a contemporary of Auschwitz, Hiroshima, Vietnam, and the Watts riots," he knew he must speak out. And speak out he did. Beginning in the summer of 1961, fired by a passion for peace, he began addressing what he considered the most urgent moral issue of his day: war. He read the signs of the times with eyes opened by contemplation and was appalled by the violence he saw at Auschwitz and Hiroshima, in Vietnam and Latin America, in Eastern Europe and the United States. He recognized that the roots of violence lay in fear and hatred and the roots of peace lay in compassion and love. He had already called readers to awaken to the reality of God deep within. Now he challenged them to live out the implications of that contemplative vision in compassion.

This chapter begins on a personal note with Merton's account of his transforming vision at a street corner in Louisville and of

*his sense of mission to work for peace. In the selections that fol-
low, we read Merton's incisive reflections on Auschwitz and the
Holocaust, on the war crisis of the early sixties, on racism and
colonialism, and on the Vietnam War. We explore, with him,
the roots of violence and war and hear his challenge to live in
nonviolence and peace.*

A TRANSFORMING VISION

*Merton's epiphany at Fourth and Walnut on March 18, 1958,
symbolized a turning point in his self-understanding and his
sense of mission. He recorded the experience in his journal
and expanded his account of it in* Conjectures of a Guilty
Bystander.

In Louisville, at the corner of Fourth and Walnut, in the center
of the shopping district, I was suddenly overwhelmed with the
realization that I loved all those people, that they were mine and
I theirs, that we could not be alien to one another even though
we were total strangers. It was like waking from a dream of
separateness, of spurious self-isolation in a special world, the
world of renunciation and supposed holiness. The whole illusion of a separate holy existence is a dream. Not that I question
the reality of my vocation, or of my monastic life: but the conception of "separation from the world" that we have in the
monastery too easily presents itself as a complete illusion: the
illusion that by making vows we become a different species of
being, pseudo-angels, "spiritual men," men of interior life, what
have you.

Certainly these traditional values are very real, but their reality is not of an order outside everyday existence in a contingent
world, nor does it entitle one to despise the secular: though "out
of the world" we are in the same world as everybody else, the
world of the bomb, the world of race hatred, the world of tech-

nology, the world of mass media, big business, revolution, and all the rest. We take a different attitude to all these things, for we belong to God. Yet so does everybody else belong to God. We just happen to be conscious of it, and to make a profession out of this consciousness. But does that entitle us to consider ourselves different, or even *better,* than others? The whole idea is preposterous.

This sense of liberation from an illusory difference was such a relief and such a joy to me that I almost laughed out loud. And I suppose my happiness could have taken form in the words: "Thank God, thank God that I *am* like other men, that I am only a man among others." To think that for sixteen or seventeen years I have been taking seriously this pure illusion that is implicit in so much of our monastic thinking.

It is a glorious destiny to be a member of the human race, though it is a race dedicated to many absurdities and one which makes many terrible mistakes: yet, with all that, God Himself gloried in becoming a member of the human race. A member of the human race! To think that such a commonplace realization should suddenly seem like news that one holds the winning ticket in a cosmic sweepstake.

I have the immense joy of being *man,* a member of a race in which God Himself became incarnate. As if the sorrows and stupidities of the human condition could overwhelm me, now I realize what we all are. And if only everybody could realize this! But it cannot be explained. There is no way of telling people that they are all walking around shining like the sun.

This changes nothing in the sense and value of my solitude, for it is in fact the function of solitude to make one realize such things with a clarity that would be impossible to anyone completely immersed in the other cares, the other illusions, and all the automatisms of a tightly collective existence. My solitude, however, is not my own, for I see now how much it belongs to them — and that I have a responsibility for it in their regard, not just in my own. It is because I am one with them that I owe it to them to be alone, and when I am alone they are not "they" but my own self. There are no strangers!

Then it was as if I suddenly saw the secret beauty of their hearts, the depths of their hearts where neither sin nor desire nor self-knowledge can reach, the core of their reality, the person that each one is in God's eyes. If only they could all see themselves as they really *are*. If only we could see each other that way all the time. There would be no more war, no more hatred, no more cruelty, no more greed.... I suppose the big problem would be that we would fall down and worship each other. But this cannot be *seen*, only believed and "understood" by a peculiar gift.   — CGB 156–58

FROM VISION TO MISSION

It seems to me that, as a contemplative, I do not need to lock myself into solitude and lose all contact with the rest of the world; rather this poor world has a right to a place in my solitude. It is not enough for me to think of the apostolic value of prayer and penance; I also have to think in terms of a contemplative grasp of the political, intellectual, artistic, and social movements in this world — by which I mean a sympathy for the honest aspirations of so many intellectuals everywhere in the world and the terrible problems they have to face. I have had the experience of seeing that this kind of understanding and friendly sympathy, on the part of a monk who really understands them, has produced striking effects among artists, writers, publishers, poets, etc., who have become my friends without my having to leave the cloister. I have even been in correspondence with the Russian writer who won the Nobel Prize in Literature, Boris Pasternak. This was before the tragic change in his situation. We got to understand one another very well. In short, with the approval of my Superiors, I have exercised an apostolate — small and limited though it be — within a circle of intellectuals from other parts of the world; and it has been quite simply an apostolate of friendship.

—Letter to Pope John XXIII,
November 10, 1958, HGL 482

•

...I don't feel that I can in conscience, at a time like this, go on writing just about things like meditation, though that has its point. I cannot just bury my head in a lot of rather tiny and secondary monastic studies either. I think I have to face the big issues, the life-and-death issues.

—Letter to Dorothy Day, August 23, 1961, HGL 140

•

One thing that has kept me very busy in the last few weeks is the international crisis. It is not really my business to speak out about it, but since there is such frightful apathy and passivity everywhere, with people simply unable to face the issue squarely, and with only a stray voice raised tentatively here and there, it has become an urgent obligation. This has kept me occupied and will keep me even more occupied, because I am now perfectly convinced that there is one task for me that takes precedence over everything else: working with such means as I have at my disposal for the abolition of war. This is like going into the prize ring blindfolded and with hands tied, since I am cloistered and subject to the most discouragingly long and frustrating kinds of censorship on top of it. I must do what I can. Prayer of course remains my chief means, but it is also an obligation on my part to speak out insofar as I am able, and to speak as clearly, as forthrightly and as uncompromisingly as I can. A lot of people are not going to like this and it may mean my head, so do please pray for me in a very special way, because I cannot in conscience willingly betray the truth or let it be betrayed. The issue is too serious. This is purely and simply the crucifixion over again. Those who think there

can be a just cause for measures that gravely risk leading to
the destruction of the entire human race are in the most dangerous illusion, and if they are Christian they are purely and
simply arming themselves with hammer and nails, without realizing it, to crucify and deny Christ. The extent of our spiritual
obtuseness is reaching a frightful scale. Of course there is in it
all a great mercy of God Whose Word descends like the rain
and snow from heaven and cannot return to Him empty: but
the demonic power at work in history is appalling, especially in
these last months. We are reaching a moment of greatest crisis,
through the blindness and stupidity of our leaders and all who
believe in them and in the society we have set up for ourselves,
and which is falling apart.

— Letter to Etta Gullick, October 1961, HGL 346-47

•

That I should have been born in 1915, that I should be the contemporary of Auschwitz, Hiroshima, Vietnam, and the Watts
riots, are things about which I was not first consulted. Yet they
are also events in which, whether I like it or not, I am deeply
and personally involved. The "world" is not just a physical
space traversed by jet planes and full of people running in all
directions. It is a complex of responsibilities and options made
out of the loves, the hates, the fears, the joys, the hopes, the
greed, the cruelty, the kindness, the faith, the trust, the suspicion
of all. In the last analysis, if there is war because nobody trusts
anybody, this is in part because I myself am defensive, suspicious, untrusting, and intent on making other people conform
themselves to my particular brand of death wish.

— "Is the World a Problem?" CWA 161

A SEASON OF FURY

The world is in crisis. A kind of madness sweeps through human society, threatening to destroy it altogether.
                                    — "Preface to the Korean Edition
                                    of *Life and Holiness*," HR 99

•

Merton wrote this poem during the summer of 1961. Published in the Catholic Worker *in August, it marked the beginning of Merton's intense period of writing on issues of war and peace in the months that followed.*

CHANT TO BE USED IN PROCESSIONS
AROUND A SITE WITH FURNACES

How he made them sleep and purified them

How we perfectly cleaned up the people and worked a big heater

I was the commander I made improvements and installed a guaranteed system taking account of human weakness I purified and I remained decent

How I commanded

I made cleaning appointments and then I made the travellers sleep and after that I made soap

I was born into a Catholic family but as these people were not going to need a priest I did not become a priest I installed a perfectly good machine it gave satisfaction to many

When trains arrived the soiled passengers received appointments for fun in the bathroom and they did not guess

It was a very big bathroom for two thousand people it awaited arrival and they arrived safely

There would be an orchestra of merry widows not all the time much art

If they arrived at all they would be given a greeting card to send home taken care of with good jobs wishing you would come to our joke

Another improvement I made was I built the chambers for two thousand invitations at a time the naked votaries were disinfected with Zyklon B

Children of tender age were always invited by reason of their youth they were unable to work they were marked out for play

They were washed like the others and more than the others

Very frequently women would hide their children in the piles of clothing but of course when we came to find them we would send the children into the chamber to be bathed

How I often commanded and made improvements and sealed the door on top there were flowers the men came with crystals I guaranteed the crystal parlor

I guaranteed the chamber and it was sealed you could see through portholes

They waited for the shower it was not hot water that came through vents though efficient winds gave full satisfaction portholes showed this

The satisfied all ran together to the doors awaiting arrival it was guaranteed they made ends meet

How I could tell by their cries that love came to a full stop I found the ones I had made clean after about a half hour

Jewish male inmates then worked up nice they had rubber boots in return for adequate food I could not guess their appetite

Those at the door were taken apart out of a fully stopped love by rubber male inmates strategic hair and teeth being used later for defense

Then the males removed all clean love rings and made away with happy gold

How I commanded and made soap 12 lbs fat 10 quarts water 8 oz to a lb of caustic soda but it was hard to find any fat

A big new firm promoted steel forks operating on a cylinder they got the contract and the faultless workmanship delivered very fast goods

"For transporting the customers we suggest using light carts on wheels a drawing is submitted"

"We acknowledge four steady furnaces and an emergency guarantee"

"I am a big new commander operating on a cylinder I elevate the purified materials boil for 2 to 3 hours and then cool"

For putting them into a test fragrance I suggested an express elevator operated by the latest cylinder it was guaranteed

Their love was fully stopped by our perfected ovens but the love rings were salvaged

Thanks to the satisfaction of male inmates operating the heaters without need of compensation our guests were warmed

All the while I had obeyed perfectly

So I was hanged in a commanding position with a full view of the site plant and grounds

You smile at my career but you would do as I did if you knew yourself and dared

In my day we worked hard we saw what we did our self sacrifice was conscientious and complete our work was faultless and
detailed

Do not think yourself better because you burn up friends and
enemies with long-range missiles without ever seeing what you
have done   —CP 345–49

•

*"A Devout Meditation in Memory of Adolf Eichmann," first
published in* Ramparts *(October 1966), exposes the deadly irony
of Eichmann's doubletalk as well as the absurd "sanity" of the
war mentality.*

One of the most disturbing facts that came out in the Eichmann
trial was that a psychiatrist examined him and pronounced him
perfectly sane. I do not doubt it at all, and this is precisely
why I find it disturbing. If all the Nazis had been psychotics,
as some of their leaders probably were, their appalling cruelty
would have been in some sense easier to understand. It is
much worse to consider this calm, "well-balanced," unper-
turbed official, conscientiously going about his desk work, his
administrative job in the great organization: which happened to
be the supervision of mass murder. He was thoughtful, orderly,
unimaginative. He had a profound respect for system, for law
and order. He was obedient, loyal, a faithful officer of a great
state. He served his government very well.

He was not bothered much by guilt. I have not heard that
he developed any psychosomatic illnesses. Apparently he slept
well. He had a good appetite, or so it seems. True, when he
visited Auschwitz, the Camp Commandant, Hoess, in a spirit
of sly deviltry, tried to tease the big boss and scare him with
some of the sights. Eichmann was disturbed, yes. He was disturbed. Even Himmler had been disturbed and had gone weak
at the knees. Perhaps, in the same way, the General Manager

of a big steel mill might be disturbed if an accident took place while he happened to be somewhere in the plant. But of course what happened at Auschwitz was not an accident: just the routine unpleasantness of the daily task. One must shoulder the burden of daily monotonous work for the Fatherland. Yes, one must suffer discomfort and even nausea from unpleasant sights and sounds. It all comes under the heading of duty, self-sacrifice, and obedience. Eichmann was devoted to duty, and proud of his job.

The sanity of Eichmann is disturbing. We equate sanity with a sense of justice, with humaneness, with prudence, with the capacity to love and understand other people. We are relying on the sane people of the world to preserve it from barbarism, madness, destruction. And now it begins to dawn on us that it is precisely the *sane* ones who are the most dangerous.

It is the sane ones, the well-adapted ones, who can without qualms and without nausea aim the missiles and press the buttons that will initiate the great festival of destruction that they, *the sane ones,* have prepared. What makes us so sure, after all, that the danger comes from a psychotic getting into a position to fire the first shot in a nuclear war? Psychotics will be suspect. The sane ones will keep them far from the button. No one suspects the sane, and the sane one will have *perfectly good reasons*, logical, well-adapted reasons, for firing the shot. They will be obeying sane orders that have come sanely down the chain of command. And because of their sanity they will have no qualms at all. When the missiles take off, then *it will be no mistake.*

In other words, then we can no longer assume that because a man is "sane" he is therefore in his "right mind." The whole concept of sanity in a society where spiritual values have lost their meaning is itself meaningless. A man can be "sane" in the limited sense that he is not impeded by his disordered emotions from acting in a cool, orderly manner, according to the needs and dictates of the social situation in which he finds himself. He can be perfectly "adjusted." God knows, perhaps such people can be perfectly adjusted even in hell itself.

And so I ask myself: what is the meaning of a concept of sanity that excludes love, considers it irrelevant, and destroys our capacity to love other human beings, to respond to their needs and their sufferings, to recognize them also as persons, to apprehend their pain as one's own? Evidently this is not necessary for "sanity" at all. It is a religious notion, a spiritual notion, a Christian notion. What business have we to equate "sanity" with "Christianity"? None at all, obviously. The worst error is to imagine that a Christian must try to be "sane" like everybody else, and that we *belong* in our kind of *society*. That we must be "realistic" about it. We must develop a *sane* Christianity: and there have been plenty of sane Christians in the past. Torture is nothing new, is it? We ought to be able to rationalize a little bit of brainwashing, and genocide, and find a place for nuclear war in our moral theology. Certainly some of us are doing our best along those lines already. There are hopes! Even Christians can shake off their sentimental prejudices about charity, and become sane like Eichmann. They can even cling to a certain set of Christian formulas, and fit them into a Totalist Ideology. Let them talk about justice, charity, love, and the rest. These words have not stopped some sane men from acting very sanely and cleverly in the past....

No, Eichmann was sane. The generals and fighters on both sides, in World War II, the ones who carried out the total destruction of entire cities, these were the sane ones. The ones who have invented and developed atomic bombs, thermonuclear bombs, missiles, who have planned the strategy of the next war; who have evaluated the various possibilities of using bacterial and chemical agents: these are not the crazy people, they are the *sane* people. The ones who coolly estimate how many millions of victims can be considered expendable in a nuclear war, I presume they do all right with the Rorschach ink blots too. On the other hand, you will probably find that the pacifists and the ban-the-bomb people are, quite seriously, just as we read in *Time,* a little crazy.

I am beginning to realize that "sanity" is no longer a value or an end in itself. The "sanity" of modern man is about as useful to him as the huge bulk and muscles of the dinosaur. If he were a little less sane, a little more doubtful, a little more aware of his absurdities and contradictions, perhaps there might be a possibility of his survival. But if he is sane, too sane . . . or perhaps we must say that in a society like ours the worst insanity is to be totally without anxiety, totally "sane."

> — "A Devout Meditation in Memory of
> Adolf Eichmann," PP 199–201

•

While he was reading Bernd Naumann's Auschwitz,* *Merton listed in his notebook some of the euphemisms that concealed the "reality" of the Auschwitz murder machine. The following are excerpts from Merton's review of Naumann's book, first published in the* Catholic Worker *(November 1967).*

Language itself has fallen victim to total war, genocide, and systematic tyranny in our time. In destroying human beings, and human values, on a mass scale, the Gestapo also subjected the German language to violence and crude perversion.

In Auschwitz secrecy was emphasized. "If you talk about what they can see from here," one prisoner was told, "you'll go through the chimney." Written records were kept cryptic, evasive. Great care was taken to destroy as much paperwork as possible before the Russians arrived. Even mention of corporal punishment was taboo. Any open reference to the realities of life and death in the camp was regarded as treason. Any

---

*Bernd Naumann, *Auschwitz: A Report on the Proceedings against Robert Karl Ludwig Mulka and Others before the Court of Frankfurt,* translated by Jean Steinberg, with an introduction by Hannah Arendt (London: Pall Mall Press, 1966).

guard, doctor, prison administrator who let out the truth could be severely punished for "defeatist talk."

This circumlocution itself was highly significant. It admitted the sinister and ironic fact that even knowledge of the truth about Auschwitz could furnish a formidable propaganda weapon to the enemies of the Reich. The very irony of the fact should have raised some urgent questions about the principle behind the camp. But the function of doubletalk and doublethink is to say everything without raising inconvenient questions. Officialese has a talent for discussing reality while denying it and calling truth itself into question. Yet the truth remains. This doubletalk is by its very nature invested with a curious metaphysical leer. The language of Auschwitz is one of the vulnerable spots through which we get a clear view of the demonic.

Gestapo doubletalk encircles reality as a doughnut encircles its hole. "Special treatment," "special housing." We need no more than one lesson, and we gain the intuition which identifies the hole, the void of death, in the heart of the expression. When the circumlocution becomes a little more insistent ("recovery camps for the tired") it brings with it suggestions of awful lassitude, infinite hopelessness, as if meaning had now been abolished forever and we were definitively at the mercy of the absurd.

"Disinfectants," "materials for the resettlement of Jews," "ovaltine substitute from the Swiss Red Cross" — all references to Zyklon B! When a deadly poison gas is referred to as soothing, restorative, a quasi-medicine to put babies to sleep, one senses behind the phrase a deep hatred of life itself. The key to Auschwitz language is its pathological joy in death. This turns out to be the key to all officialese. All of it is the celebration of boredom, of routine, of deadness, or organized futility. Auschwitz just carried the whole thing to its logical extreme, with a kind of heavy lilt in its mockery, its oafish love of death....

One of the results of the Frankfurt trial is that it makes an end of the pure Auschwitz myth: the myth of demented monsters who were twice our size, with six eyes and four rows of teeth, not of the same world as ourselves. The demonic sickness of Auschwitz emanated from ordinary people, stimulated by an extraordinary regime....

Salutary Reflections

Such is the first conclusion. We have learned to associate the incredible brutality and inhumanity of Auschwitz with ordinary respectable people, in an extraordinary situation.

Second: Auschwitz worked because these people wanted it to work. Instead of resisting it, rebelling against it, they put the best of their energies into making genocide a success. This was true not only of one or two psychopaths but of an entire bureaucratic officialdom, including not only the secret police and Nazi party members but also managers and employees of the industries which knowingly made use of the slave labor provided in such abundance by the camp.

Third: although it was usual to argue that "they had no choice" and that they were "forced" to comply with orders, the trial showed a more complex and less excusable picture of the defendants. Almost all of them committed gratuitous acts of arbitrary cruelty and violence which were forbidden even by the Gestapo's own rules. Some were even punished by the SS for these violations. Was there no choice? There are on record refusals of men who simply would not take part in murder and got themselves transferred. Why was this not done more often? Let us clearly spell out two of the circumstances. Auschwitz was safe. One was not at the front, and there was practically no danger from bombing planes. And there were privileges: the work was no doubt disagreeable to some, but there were extra rations, smokes, drinks. Finally, there can be little doubt that many of these men tortured and killed because they thoroughly enjoyed it.

Fourth: what does all this add up to? Given the right situation and another Hitler, places like Auschwitz can be set up, put into action, kept running smoothly, with thousands of people systematically starved, beaten, gassed, and whole crematories going full blast. Such camps can be set up tomorrow anywhere and made to work with the greatest efficiency, because there is no dearth of people who would be glad to do the job, provided it is sanctioned by authority. They will be glad because they will instinctively welcome and submit to an ideology which enables them to be violent and destructive without guilt. They are happy with a belief which turns them loose against their fellow man to destroy him cruelly and without compunction, as long as he belongs to a different race, or believes in a different set of semi-meaningless political slogans.

It is enough to affirm one basic principle: ANYONE BELONGING TO CLASS X OR NATION Y OR RACE Z IS TO BE REGARDED AS SUBHUMAN AND WORTHLESS, AND CONSEQUENTLY HAS NO RIGHT TO EXIST. All the rest will follow without difficulty.

As long as this principle is easily available, as long as it is taken for granted, as long as it can be spread out on the front pages at a moment's notice and accepted by all, we have no need of monsters: ordinary policemen and good citizens will take care of everything.

— "Auschwitz: A Family Camp," PP 281–86

THE ROOTS OF HATE AND VIOLENCE

Merton wrote these paragraphs as an introduction to chapter 16 of New Seeds of Contemplation, *which he sent to Dorothy Day for publication in the* Catholic Worker. *Although the censors had approved* New Seeds, *Merton did not submit the introductory paragraphs for their approval. The publication of "The Root of War Is Fear," with the uncensored introductory material in*

October 1961, signaled what William H. Shannon has termed Merton's "definitive entry" into the struggle against war.

The present war crisis is something we have made entirely for and by ourselves. There is in reality not the slightest logical reason for war, and yet the whole world is plunging headlong into frightful destruction, and doing so *with the purpose of avoiding war and preserving peace!* This is a true war-madness, an illness of the mind and the spirit that is spreading with a furious and subtle contagion all over the world. Of all the countries that are sick, America is perhaps the most grievously afflicted. On all sides we have people building bomb shelters where, in case of nuclear war, they will simply bake slowly instead of burning up quickly or being blown out of existence in a flash. And they are prepared to sit in these shelters with machine guns with which to prevent their neighbor from entering. This is a nation that claims to be fighting for religious truth along with freedom and other values of the spirit. Truly we have entered the "post-Christian era" with a vengeance. Whether we are destroyed or whether we survive, the future is awful to contemplate.

The Christian

What is the place of the Christian in all this? Is he simply to fold his hands and resign himself to the worst, accepting it as the inescapable will of God and preparing himself to enter heaven with a sigh of relief? Should he open up the Apocalypse and run out into the street to give everyone his idea of what is happening? Or worse still, should he take a hard-headed and "practical" attitude about it and join in the madness of the warmakers, calculating how by a "first strike," the glorious Christian West can eliminate atheistic communism for all time and usher in the millennium?...I am no prophet and no seer but it seems to me that this last position may very well be the most diabolical of illusions, the great and not even subtle temptation of a Christianity that has grown rich and comfortable, and is satisfied with its riches.

What are we to do? The duty of the Christian in this crisis is to strive with all his power and intelligence, with his faith, hope in Christ, and love for God and man, to do the one task which God has imposed upon us in the world today. That task is to work for total abolition of war. *There can be no question that unless war is abolished the world will remain constantly in a state of madness and desperation in which, because of the immense destructive power of modern weapons, the danger of catastrophe will be imminent and probably at every moment everywhere.* Unless we set ourselves immediately to this task, both as individuals and in our political and religious groups, we tend by our passivity and fatalism to cooperate with the destructive forces that are leading inexorably to war. It is a problem of terrifying complexity and magnitude, for which the Church herself is not fully able to see clear and decisive solutions. Yet she must lead the way on the road towards nonviolent settlement of difficulties and towards the gradual abolition of war as a way of settling international or civil disputes. Christians must become active in every possible way, mobilizing all their resources for the fight against war. First of all there is much to be studied, much to be learned. Peace is to be preached, nonviolence is to be explained as a practical method, and not left to be mocked as an outlet for crackpots who want to make a show of themselves. Prayer and sacrifice must be used as the most effective spiritual weapons in the war against war, and like all weapons they must be used with deliberate aim: not just with a vague aspiration for peace and security, but against violence and against war. This implies that we are also willing to sacrifice and restrain our own instinct for violence and aggressiveness in our relations with other people. We may never succeed in this campaign but whether we succeed or not the duty is evident. It is the great Christian task of our time. Everything else is secondary, for the survival of the human race itself depends on it. We must at least face this responsibility and do something about it. And the first job of all is to understand the psychological forces at work in ourselves and in society.

— "The Root of War," *Catholic Worker,*
October 1961, PP 11–13

Chapter 16 of New Seeds of Contemplation

At the root of all war is fear: not so much the fear men have of one another as the fear they have of *everything*. It is not merely that they do not trust one another; they do not even trust themselves. If they are not sure when someone else may turn around and kill them, they are still less sure when they may turn around and kill themselves. They cannot trust anything, because they have ceased to believe in God.

It is not only our hatred of others that is dangerous but also and above all our hatred of ourselves: particularly that hatred of ourselves which is too deep and too powerful to be consciously faced. For it is this which makes us see our own evil in others and unable to see it in ourselves.

When we see crime in others, we try to correct it by destroying them or at least putting them out of sight. It is easy to identify the sin with the sinner when he is someone other than our own self. In ourselves, it is the other way round; we see the sin, but we have great difficulty in shouldering responsibility for it. We find it very hard to identify our sin with our own will and our own malice. On the contrary, we naturally tend to interpret our immoral act as an involuntary mistake, or as the malice of a spirit in us that is other than ourself. Yet at the same time we are fully aware that others do not make this convenient distinction for us. The acts that have been done by us are, in their eyes, "our" acts and they hold us fully responsible.

What is more, we tend unconsciously to ease ourselves still more of the burden of guilt that is in us, by passing it on to somebody else. When I have done wrong, and have excused myself by attributing the wrong to "another" who is unaccountably "in me," my conscience is not yet satisfied. There is still too much left to be explained. The "other in myself" is too close to home. The temptation is, then, to account for my fault by seeing an equivalent amount of evil in someone else. Hence I minimize my own sins and compensate for doing so by exaggerating the faults of others.

As if this were not enough, we make the situation much worse by artificially intensifying our sense of evil, and by increasing our propensity to feel guilt even for things which are not in themselves wrong. In all these ways we build up such an obsession with evil, both in ourselves and in others, that we waste all our mental energy trying to account for this evil, to punish it, to exorcise it, or to get rid of it in any way we can. We drive ourselves mad with our preoccupation and in the end there is no outlet left but violence. We have to destroy something or someone. By that time we have created for ourselves a suitable enemy, a scapegoat in whom we have invested all the evil in the world. He is the cause of every wrong. He is the fomenter of all conflict. If he can only be destroyed, conflict will cease, evil will be done with, there will be no more war....

When the whole world is in moral confusion, when no one knows any longer what to think, and when, in fact, everybody is running away from the responsibility of thinking, when man makes rational thought about moral issues absurd by exiling himself entirely from realities into the realm of fictions, and when he expends all his efforts in constructing more fictions with which to account for his ethical failures, then it becomes clear that the world cannot be saved from global war and global destruction by the mere efforts and good intentions of peacemakers. In actual fact, everyone is becoming more and more aware of the widening gulf between good purposes and bad results, between efforts to make peace and the growing likelihood of war. It seems that no matter how elaborate and careful the planning, all attempts at international dialogue end in more and more ludicrous failures. In the end no one has any more faith in those who even attempt the dialogue. On the contrary, the negotiators, with all their pathetic good will, become the objects of contempt and of hatred. It is the "men of good will," the men who have made their poor efforts to do something about peace, who will in the end be the most mercilessly reviled, crushed, and destroyed as victims of the universal self-hate of man which they have unfortunately only increased by the failure of their good intentions.

Perhaps we still have a basically superstitious tendency to associate failure with dishonesty and guilt — failure being interpreted as "punishment." Even if a man starts out with good intentions, if he fails we tend to think he was somehow "at fault." If he was not guilty, he was at least "wrong." And "being wrong" is something we have not yet learned to face with equanimity and understanding. We either condemn it with godlike disdain or forgive it with god-like condescension. We do not manage to accept it with human compassion, humility, and identification. Thus we never see the one truth that would help us begin to solve our ethical and political problems: that we are *all* more or less wrong, that we are *all* at fault, *all* limited and obstructed by our mixed motives, our self-deception, our greed, our self-righteousness, and our tendency to aggressivity and hypocrisy.

In our refusal to accept the partially good intentions of others and work with them (of course prudently and with resignation to the inevitable imperfection of the result) we are unconsciously proclaiming our own malice, our own intolerance, our own lack of realism, our own ethical and political quackery.

Perhaps in the end the first real step toward peace would be a realistic acceptance of the fact that our political ideals are perhaps to a great extent illusions and fictions to which we cling out of motives that are not always perfectly honest: that because of this we prevent ourselves from seeing any good or any practicability in the political ideals of our enemies — which may, of course, be in many ways even more illusory and dishonest than our own. We will never get anywhere unless we can accept the fact that politics is an inextricable tangle of good and evil motives in which, perhaps, the evil predominate but where one must continue to hope doggedly in what little good can still be found.

But someone will say: "If we recognize that we are all equally wrong, all political action will instantly be paralyzed. We can only act when we assume that we are in the right." On the contrary, I believe the basis for valid political action can only be the recognition that the true solution to our problems is *not* accessible to any one isolated party or nation but that all must arrive at it by working together.

I do not mean to encourage the guilt-ridden thinking that is always too glad to be "wrong" in everything. This too is an evasion of responsibility, because every form of oversimplification tends to make decisions ultimately meaningless. We must try to accept ourselves, whether individually or collectively, not only as perfectly good or perfectly bad, but in our mysterious, unaccountable mixture of good and evil. We have to stand by the modicum of good that is in us without exaggerating it. We have to defend our real rights, because unless we respect our own rights we will certainly not respect the rights of others. But at the same time we have to recognize that we have willfully or otherwise trespassed on the rights of others. We must be able to admit this not only as the result of self-examination, but when it is pointed out unexpectedly, and perhaps not too gently, by somebody else.

These principles which govern personal moral conduct, which make harmony possible in small social units like the family, also apply in the wider area of the state and in the whole community of nations. It is, however, quite absurd, in our present situation or in any other, to expect these principles to be universally accepted as the result of moral exhortations. There is very little hope that the world will be run according to them, all of a sudden, as a result of some hypothetical change of heart on the part of politicians. It is useless and even laughable to base political thought on the faint hope of a purely contingent and subjective moral illumination in the hearts of the world's leaders. But outside of political thought and action, in the religious sphere, it is not only permissible to hope for such a mysterious consummation, but it is necessary to pray for it. We can and must believe not so much that the mysterious light of God can "convert" the ones who are mostly responsible for the world's peace, but at least that they may, in spite of their obstinacy and their prejudices, be guarded against fatal error.

It would be sentimental folly to expect men to trust one another when they obviously cannot be trusted. But at least they can learn to trust God. They can bring themselves to see that the mysterious power of God can, quite independently of human malice and error, protect men unaccountably against themselves, and that He can always turn evil into good, though perhaps not always in a sense that would be understood by preachers of sunshine and uplift. If they can trust and love God, Who is infinitely wise and Who rules the lives of men, permitting them to use their freedom even to the point of almost incredible abuse, they can love men who are evil. They can learn to love them even in their sin, as God has loved them. If we can love the men we cannot trust (without trusting them foolishly) and if we can to some extent share the burden of their sin by identifying ourselves with them, then perhaps there is some hope of a kind of peace on earth, based not on the wisdom and the manipulations of men but on the inscrutable mercy of God.

For only love — which means humility — can exorcise the fear which is at the root of all war.

What is the use of postmarking our mail with exhortations to "pray for peace" and then spending billions of dollars on atomic submarines, thermonuclear weapons, and ballistic missiles? This, I would think, would certainly be what the New Testament calls "mocking God" — and mocking Him far more effectively than the atheists do. The culminating horror of the joke is that we are piling up these weapons to protect ourselves against atheists who, quite frankly, believe there is no God and are convinced that one has to rely on bombs and missiles since nothing else offers any real security. Is it then because we have so much trust in the power of God that we are intent upon utterly destroying these people before they can destroy us? Even at the risk of destroying ourselves at the same time?

I do not mean to imply that prayer excludes the simultaneous use of ordinary human means to accomplish a naturally good and justifiable end. One can very well pray for a restoration of physical health and at the same time take medicine prescribed by a doctor. In fact, a believer should normally do both. And there would seem to be a reasonable and right proportion between the use of these two means to the same end.

But consider the utterly fabulous amount of money, planning, energy, anxiety, and care which go into the production of weapons which almost immediately become obsolete and have to be scrapped. Contrast all this with the pitiful little gesture "pray for peace" piously canceling our four-cent stamps! Think, too, of the disproportion between our piety and the enormous act of murderous destruction which we at the same time countenance without compunction and without shame! It does not even seem to enter our minds that there might be some incongruity in praying to the God of peace, the God Who told us to love one another as He had loved us, Who warned us that they who took the sword would perish by it, and at the same time planning to annihilate not thousands but millions of civilians and soldiers, men, women, and children without discrimination, even with the almost infallible certainty of inviting the same annihilation for ourselves!

It may make sense for a sick man to pray for health and then take medicine, but I fail to see any sense at all in his praying for health and then drinking poison.

When I pray for peace I pray God to pacify not only the Russians and the Chinese but above all my own nation and myself. When I pray for peace I pray to be protected not only from the Reds but also from the folly and blindness of my own country. When I pray for peace, I pray not only that the enemies of my country may cease to want war, but above all that my own country will cease to do the things that make war inevitable. In other words, when I pray for peace I am not just praying that the Russians will give up without a struggle and let us have our own way. I am praying that both we and the Russians may somehow be restored to sanity and learn how to work out our problems, as best we can, together, instead of preparing for global suicide.

I am fully aware that this sounds utterly sentimental, archaic, and out of tune with an age of science. But I would like to submit that pseudo-scientific thinking in politics and sociology have so far had much less than this to offer. One thing I would like to add in all fairness is that the atomic scientists themselves are quite often the ones most concerned about the ethics of the situation, and that they are among the few who dare to open their mouths from time to time and say something about it.

But who on earth listens?

If men really wanted peace they would sincerely ask God for it and He would give it to them. But why should He give the world a peace which it does not really desire? The peace the world pretends to desire is really no peace at all.

To some men peace merely means the liberty to exploit other people without fear of retaliation or interference. To others peace means the freedom to rob others without interruption. To still others it means the leisure to devour the goods of the earth without being compelled to interrupt their pleasures to feed those whom their greed is starving. And to practically everybody peace simply means the absence of any physical violence that might cast a shadow over lives devoted to the satisfaction of their animal appetites for comfort and pleasure.

Many men like these have asked God for what they thought was "peace" and wondered why their prayer was not answered. They could not understand that it actually *was* answered. God left them with what they desired, for their idea of peace was only another form of war. The "cold war" is simply the normal consequence of our corrupt idea of a peace based on a policy of "every man for himself" in ethics, economics, and political life. It is absurd to hope for a solid peace based on fictions and illusions!

So instead of loving what you think is peace, love other men and love God above all. And instead of hating the people you think are warmakers, hate the appetites and the disorder in your own soul, which are the causes of war. If you love peace, then hate injustice, hate tyranny, hate greed — but hate these things *in yourself,* not in another.   —NS 112–22

WE ARE ONE

I cannot treat other men as men unless I have compassion for them. I must have at least enough compassion to realize that when they suffer they feel somewhat as I do when I suffer. And if for some reason I do not spontaneously feel this kind of sympathy for others, then it is God's will that I do what I can to learn how. I must learn to share with others their joys, their sufferings, their ideas, their needs, their desires. I must learn to do this not only in the cases of those who are of the same class, the same profession, the same race, the same nation as myself, but when men who suffer belong to other groups, even to groups that are regarded as hostile. If I do this, I obey God. If I refuse to do it, I disobey Him.   —NS 76–77

•

Compassion teaches me that my brother and I are one. That if I love my brother, then my love benefits my own life as well, and if I hate my brother and seek to destroy him, I seek to destroy myself also. The desire to kill is like the desire to attack another with an ingot of red hot iron: I have to pick up the incandescent metal and burn my own hand while burning the other. Hate itself is the seed of death in my own heart, while it seeks the death of the other. Love is the seed of life in my own heart when it seeks the good of the other. . . .

Violence rests on the assumption that the enemy and I are entirely different: the enemy is evil and I am good. The enemy must be destroyed but I must be saved. But love sees things differently. It sees that even the enemy suffers from the same sorrows and limitations that I do. That we both have the same hopes, the same needs, the same aspiration for a peaceful and harmless human life. And that death is the same for both of us. Then love may perhaps show me that my brother is not really my enemy and that war is both his enemy and mine. War is *our* enemy. Then peace becomes possible.

It is true, political problems are not solved by love and mercy. But the world of politics is not the only world, and unless political decisions rest on a foundation of something better and higher than politics, they can never do any real good for men. When a country has to be rebuilt after war, the passions and energies of war are no longer enough. There must be a new force, the power of love, the power of understanding and human compassion, the strength of selflessness and cooperation, and the creative dynamism of *the will to live and to build, and the will to forgive. The will for reconciliation.*

The principles given in this book [*No Man Is an Island*] are simple and more or less traditional. They are the principles derived from religious wisdom, which, in the present case, is Christian. But many of these principles run parallel to the ancient teachings of Buddhism. They are in fact in large part universal truths. They are truths with which, for centuries, man has slowly and with difficulty built a civilized world in the effort to make happiness possible; not merely by making life materially better, but by helping men *to understand and live their life more fruitfully.*

The key to this understanding is the truth that "No man is an island." A selfish life cannot be fruitful. It cannot be true. It contradicts the very nature of man. The dire effect of this contradiction cannot be avoided; where men live selfishly, in quest of brute power and lust and money, they destroy one another. The only way to change such a world is to change the thoughts and desires of the men who live in it. The conditions of our world are simply an outward expression of our thoughts and desires....

We must all believe in love and in peace. We must believe in the power of love. We must recognize that our being itself is grounded in love; that is to say, that we come into being because we are loved and because we are meant to love others. The failure to believe this and to live accordingly creates instead a deep mistrust, a suspicion of others, a hatred of others, a failure to love. When a man attempts to live by and for himself alone, he becomes a little "island" of hate, greed, suspicion, fear, desire. Then his whole outlook on life is falsified. All his judgments are affected by that untruth. In order to recover the true perspective, which is that of love and compassion, he must once again learn, in simplicity, truth, and peace, that "No man is an island."

> — "Preface to the Vietnamese edition of
> No Man Is an Island," HR 123–26.

FAITH AND VIOLENCE

In 1968, Merton published Faith and Violence, *a collection of essays on a variety of social and religious issues: resistance and nonviolence, the war in Vietnam, the racial crisis and issues of belief and unbelief. He subtitled the book* Christian Teaching and Christian Practice. *Merton's preface to* Faith and Violence *and his opening essay "Toward a Theology of Resistance" appear below.*

The Hassidic Rabbi Baal-Shem-Tov once told the following story. Two men were traveling through a forest. One was drunk, the other was sober. As they went, they were attacked by robbers, beaten, robbed of all they had, even their clothing. When they emerged, people asked them if they got through the wood without trouble. The drunken man said: "Everything was fine; nothing went wrong; we had no trouble at all!"

They said: "How does it happen that you are naked and covered with blood?"

He did not have an answer.

The sober man said: "Do not believe him: he is drunk. It was a disaster. Robbers beat us without mercy and took everything we had. Be warned by what happened to us, and look out for yourselves."

For some "faithful" — and for unbelievers too — "faith" seems to be a kind of drunkenness, an anesthetic, that keeps you from realizing and believing that anything can ever go wrong. Such faith can be immersed in a world of violence and make no objection: the violence is perfectly all right. It is quite normal — unless of course it happens to be exercised by Negroes. Then it must be put down instantly by superior force. The drunkenness of this kind of faith — whether in a religious message or merely in a political ideology — enables us to go through life without seeing that our own violence is a disaster and that the overwhelming force by which we seek to assert ourselves and our own self-interest may well be our ruin.

Is faith a narcotic dream in a world of heavily-armed robbers, or is it an awakening?

Is faith a convenient nightmare in which we are attacked and obliged to destroy our attackers?

What if we awaken to discover that *we* are the robbers, and our destruction comes from the root of hate in ourselves?

—Preface, FV ix–x

Toward a Theology of Resistance

Theology today needs to focus carefully upon the crucial problem of violence. The commandment "Thou shalt not kill" is more than a mere matter of academic or sentimental interest in an age when man not only is more frustrated, more crowded, more subject to psychotic and hostile delusion than ever, but also has at his disposition an arsenal of weapons that make global suicide an easy possibility. But the so-called "nuclear umbrella" has not simplified matters in the least: it may (at least temporarily) have caused the nuclear powers to reconsider their impulses to reduce one another to radioactive dust. But meanwhile "conventional" wars go on with unabated cruelty, and already more bombs have been exploded on Vietnam than were dropped in the whole of World War II. The population of the affluent world is nourished on a steady diet of brutal mythology and hallucination, kept at a constant pitch of high tension by a life that is intrinsically violent in that it forces a large part of the population to submit to an existence which is humanly intolerable. Hence murder, mugging, rape, crime, corruption. But it must be remembered that the crime that breaks out of the ghetto is only the fruit of a greater and more pervasive violence: the injustice which forces people to live in the ghetto in the first place. The problem of violence, then, is not the problem of a few rioters and rebels, but the problem of a whole structure which is outwardly ordered and respectable, and inwardly ridden by psychopathic obsessions and delusions.

It is perfectly true that violence must at times be restrained by force: but a convenient mythology which simply legalizes the use of force by big criminals against little criminals — whose small-scale criminality is largely *caused* by the large-scale injustice under which they live — only perpetuates the disorder.

Pope John XXIII in *Pacem in Terris* quoted, with approval, a famous saying of St. Augustine: "What are kingdoms without justice but large bands of robbers?" The problem of violence today must be traced to its root: not the small-time murders but the massively organized bands of murderers whose operations are global....

The Catholic moral theology of war has, especially since the

Renaissance, concerned itself chiefly with casuistical discussion of how far the monarch or the sovereign state can justly make use of force. The historic context of this discussion was the struggle for a European balance of power, waged for absolute monarchs by small professional armies. In a new historical context we find not only a new struggle on a global scale between mammoth nuclear powers provided with arsenals capable of wiping out the human race, but also the emergence of scores of small nations in an undeveloped world that was until recently colonial. In this Third World we find not huge armed establishments but petty dictatorships (representing a rich minority) armed by the great powers, opposed by small, volunteer guerilla bands fighting for "the poor." The Great Powers tend to intervene in these struggles, not so much by the threat and use of nuclear weapons (with which however they continue to threaten one another) but with armies of draftees and with new experimental weapons which are sometimes incredibly savage and cruel and which are used mostly against helpless noncombatants. Although many Churchmen, moved apparently by force of habit, continue to issue mechanical blessings upon these draftees and upon the versatile applications of science to the art of killing, it is evident that this use of force does not become moral just because the government and the mass media have declared the cause to be patriotic. The cliché "My country right or wrong" does not provide a satisfactory theological answer to the moral problems raised by the intervention of American power in all parts of the Third World....

The real moral issue of violence in the twentieth century is obscured by archaic and mythical presuppositions. We tend to judge violence in terms of the individual, the messy, the physically disturbing, the personally frightening. The violence we want to see restrained is the violence of the hood waiting for us in the subway or the elevator. That is reasonable, but it tends to influence us too much. It makes us think that the problem of violence is limited to this very small scale, and it makes us unable to appreciate the far greater problem of the more abstract, more global, more organized presence of violence on a massive and corporate pattern. Violence today is *white-collar violence, the systematically organized bureaucratic and technological destruction of man.*

The theology of violence must not lose sight of the real problem which is not the individual with a revolver but *death and even genocide as big business.* But this big business of death is all the more innocent and effective because it involves a long chain of individuals, each of whom can feel himself absolved from responsibility, and each of whom can perhaps salve his conscience by contributing with a more *meticulous efficiency* to his part in the massive operation.

We know, for instance, that Adolf Eichmann and others like him felt no guilt for their share in the extermination of the Jews. This feeling of justification was due partly to their absolute obedience to higher authority and partly to the care and efficiency which went into the details of their work. This was done almost entirely on paper. Since they dealt with numbers, not with people, and since their job was one of abstract bureaucratic organization, apparently they could easily forget the reality of what they were doing. The same is true to an even greater extent in modern warfare in which the real moral problems are not to be located in rare instances of hand-to-hand combat, but in the remote planning and organization of technological destruction. The real crimes of modern war are committed not at the front (if any) but in war offices and ministries of defense in which no one ever has to see any blood unless his secretary gets a nosebleed. Modern technological mass murder is not directly visible, like individual murder. It is abstract, corporate, businesslike, cool, free of guilt-feelings and therefore a thousand times more deadly and effective than the eruption of violence out of individual hate. It is this polite, massively organized white-collar murder machine that threatens the world with destruction, not the violence of a few desperate teen-agers in a slum. But our antiquated theology myopically focused on *individual* violence alone fails to see this. It shudders at the phantasm of muggings and killings where a mess is made on our own doorstep, but blesses and canonizes the antiseptic violence of corporately organized murder because it is respectable, efficient, clean, and above all profitable....

A theology of love cannot afford to be sentimental. It cannot afford to preach edifying generalities about charity, while identifying "peace" with mere established power and legalized violence against the oppressed. A theology of love cannot be allowed merely to serve the interests of the rich and powerful, justifying their wars, their violence, and their bombs, while exhorting the poor and underprivileged to practice patience, meekness, longsuffering and to solve their problems, if at all, nonviolently.

The theology of love must seek to deal realistically with the evil and injustice in the world, and not merely to compromise with them. Such a theology will have to take note of the ambiguous realities of politics, without embracing the specious myth of a "realism" that merely justifies force in the service of established power. Theology does not exist merely to appease the already too untroubled conscience of the powerful and the established. A theology of love may also conceivably turn out to be a theology of revolution. In any case, it is a theology of *resistance,* a refusal of the evil that reduces a brother to homicidal desperation....

Such a theology could not claim to be Christian if it did not retain at least some faith in the meaning of the Cross and of the redemptive death of Jesus who, instead of using force against his accusers, took all the evil upon himself and overcame that evil by his suffering. This is a basic Christian pattern, but a realistic theology will, I believe, give a new practical emphasis to it. Instead of preaching the Cross *for others* and advising them to suffer patiently the violence which we sweetly impose on them, with the aid of armies and police, we might conceivably recognize the right of the less fortunate to use force, and study more seriously the practice of nonviolence and humane methods on our own part when, as it happens, we possess the most stupendous arsenal of power the world has ever known....

The reason for emphasizing nonviolent resistance is this: he who resists force with force in order to seize power may become contaminated by the evil which he is resisting and, when he gains power, may be just as ruthless and unjust a tyrant as the one he has dethroned. A nonviolent victory, while far more difficult to achieve, stands a better chance of curing the illness instead of contracting it.

There is an essential difference here, for nonviolence seeks to "win" not by destroying or even by humiliating the adversary, but by *convincing him* that there is a higher and more certain common good than can be attained by bombs and blood. Nonviolence, ideally speaking, does not try to overcome the adversary by winning over him, but to turn him from an adversary into a collaborator by winning him over. Unfortunately, nonviolent resistance as practiced by those who do not understand it and have not been trained in it is often only a weak and veiled form of psychological aggression.

— "Toward a Theology of Resistance," FV 3–13

THE WAY OF NONVIOLENCE

Merton wrote this essay in 1966 for German pacifist Hildegaard Goss-Mayr. She had asked Merton to write about humility. He said he would do so "in the context of nonviolence." In the resulting essay (published in Germany in 1966 and in the U.S. in 1967), "Blessed Are the Meek," Merton discusses the Christian roots of nonviolence and what the practice of nonviolence entails.

It would be a serious mistake to regard Christian nonviolence simply as a novel tactic which is at once efficacious and even edifying, and which enables the sensitive man to participate in the struggles of the world without being dirtied with blood. Non-violence is not simply a way of proving one's point and getting what one wants without being involved in behavior that one considers ugly and evil. Nor is it, for that matter, a means which anyone legitimately can make use of according to his fancy for any purpose whatever. To practice nonviolence for a purely self-ish or arbitrary end would in fact discredit and distort the truth of nonviolent resistance.

Nonviolence is perhaps the most exacting of all forms of struggle, not only because it demands first of all that one be ready to suffer evil and even face the threat of death without violent retaliation, but because it excludes mere transient self-interest from its considerations. In a very real sense, he who practices nonviolent resistance must commit himself not to the defense of his own interests or even those of a particular group: he must commit himself to the defense of objective truth and right and above all of *man*. His aim is then not simply to "pre-vail" or to prove that he is right and the adversary wrong, or to make the adversary give in and yield what is demanded of him.

Nor should the nonviolent resister be content to prove to *himself* that *he* is virtuous and right, and that *his* hands and heart are pure even though the adversary's may be evil and defiled. Still less should he seek for himself the psychological gratification of upsetting the adversary's conscience and perhaps driving him to an act of bad faith and refusal of the truth. We know that our unconscious motives may, at times, make our nonviolence a form of moral aggression and even a subtle provocation designed (without our awareness) to bring out the evil we hope to find in the adversary, and thus to justify our-selves in our own eyes and in the eyes of "decent people." Wherever there is a high moral ideal there is an attendant risk of pharisaism, and nonviolence is no exception. The basis of pharisaism is division: on one hand this morally or socially priv-ileged self and the elite to which it belongs. On the other hand, the "others," the wicked, the unenlightened, whoever they may be, Communists, capitalists, colonialists, traitors, international Jewry, racists, etc.

Christian nonviolence is not built on a presupposed division, but on the basic unity of man. It is not out for the conversion of the wicked to the ideas of the good, but for the healing and reconciliation of man with himself, man the person and man the human family.

The nonviolent resister is not fighting simply for "his" truth or for "his" pure conscience, or for the right that is on "his" side." On the contrary, both his strength and his weakness come from the fact that he is fighting for *the* truth, common to him and to the adversary, *the* right which is objective and universal. He is fighting for *everybody*.

For this very reason, as Gandhi saw, the fully consistent practice of nonviolence demands a solid metaphysical and religious basis both in being and in God. This comes *before* subjective good intentions and sincerity. For the Hindu this metaphysical basis was provided by the Vedantist doctrine of the Atman, the true transcendent Self which alone is absolutely real, and before which the empirical self of the individual must be effaced in the faithful practice of *dharma*. For the Christian, the basis of nonviolence is the Gospel message of salvation for *all* men and of the Kingdom of God to which *all* are summoned. The disciple of Christ, he who has heard the good news, the announcement of the Lord's coming and of his victory, and is aware of the definitive establishment of the Kingdom, proves his faith by the gift of his whole self to the Lord in order that *all* may enter the Kingdom. This Christian discipleship entails a certain way of acting, a *politeia*, a *conservatio*, which is proper to the Kingdom.

The great historical event, the coming of the Kingdom, is made clear and is "realized" in proportion as Christians themselves live the life of the Kingdom in the circumstances of their own place and time. The saving grace of God in the Lord Jesus is proclaimed to man existentially in the love, the openness, the simplicity, the humility, and the self-sacrifice of Christians. By their example of a truly Christian understanding of the world, expressed in a living and active application of the Christian faith to the human problems of their own time, Christians manifest the love of Christ for men (John 13:35, 17:21), and by that fact make him visibly present in the world. The religious basis of Christian nonviolence is then faith in Christ the Redeemer and obedience to his demand to love and manifest himself in us by a certain manner of acting in the world and in relation to other men. This obedience enables us to live as true citizens of the Kingdom, in which the divine mercy, the grace, favor, and redeeming love of God are active in our lives. Then the Holy Spirit will indeed "rest upon us" and act in us, not for our own good alone but for God and his Kingdom. And if the Spirit dwells in us and works in us, our lives will be continuous and progressive conversion and transformation in which we also, in some measure, help to transform others and allow ourselves to be transformed by and with others, in Christ.

The chief place in which this new mode of life is set forth in detail is the Sermon on the Mount. At the very beginning of this great inaugural discourse, the Lord numbers the beatitudes, which are the theological foundation of Christian nonviolence: Blessed are the poor in spirit...blessed are the meek (Matthew 5:3–4).

This does not mean "blessed are they who are endowed with a tranquil natural temperament, who are not easily moved to anger, who are always quiet and obedient, who do not naturally resist." Still less does it mean "blessed are they who passively submit to unjust oppression." On the contrary, we know that the "poor in spirit" are those of whom the prophets spoke, those who in the last days will be the "humble of the earth," that is to say, the oppressed who have no human weapons to rely on and who nevertheless are true to the commandments of Yahweh, and who hear the voice that tells them: "Seek jus-

tice, seek humility, perhaps you will find shelter on the day of
the Lord's wrath" (Sophonias 2:3). In other words they seek
justice in the power of truth and of God, not by the power of
man. Note that Christian meekness, which is essential to true
nonviolence, has this eschatological quality about it. It refrains
from self-assertion and from violent aggression because it sees
all things in the light of the great judgment. Hence it does not
struggle and fight merely for this or that ephemeral gain. It
struggles for the truth and the right which alone will stand in
that day when all is to be tried by fire (1 Corinthians 3:10–15).

Furthermore, Christian nonviolence and meekness imply a
particular understanding of the power of human poverty and
powerlessness when they are united with the invisible strength
of Christ. The Beatitudes indeed convey a profound existential
understanding of the dynamic of the Kingdom of God — a dynamic made clear in the parables of the mustard seed and of
the yeast. This is a dynamism of patient and secret growth, in
belief that out of the smallest, weakest, and most insignificant
seed the greatest tree will come. This is not merely a matter of
blind and arbitrary faith. The early history of the Church, the
record of the apostles and martyrs, remains to testify to this in-
herent and mysterious dynamism of the ecclesial "event" in the
world of history and time. Christian nonviolence is rooted in
this consciousness and this faith.

This aspect of Christian nonviolence is extremely important
and it gives us the key to a proper understanding of the meekness which accepts being "without strength" (*gewaltlos*) not
out of masochism, quietism, defeatism, or false passivity, but
trusting in the strength of the Lord of truth. Indeed, we repeat,
Christian nonviolence is nothing if not first of all a formal profession of faith in the Gospel message that the *Kingdom has
been established* and that the Lord of truth is indeed risen and
reigning over his Kingdom.

Faith of course tells us that we live in a time of eschatological
struggle, facing a fierce combat which marshalls all the forces of

evil and darkness against the still-invisible truth, yet this combat is already decided by the victory of Christ over death and over sin. The Christian can renounce the protection of violence and risk being humble, therefore *vulnerable,* not because he trusts in the supposed efficacy of a gentle and persuasive tactic that will disarm hatred and tame cruelty, but because he believes that the hidden power of the Gospel is demanding to be manifested in and through his own poor person. Hence in perfect obedience to the Gospel, he effaces himself and his own interests and even risks his life in order to testify not simply to "the truth" in a sweeping, idealistic, and purely platonic sense, but to the truth that is incarnate in a concrete human situation, involving living persons whose rights are denied or whose lives are threatened.

Here it must be remarked that a holy zeal for the cause of humanity in the abstract may sometimes be mere lovelessness and indifference for concrete and living human beings. When we appeal to the highest and most noble ideals, we are more easily tempted to hate and condemn those who, so we believe, are standing in the way of their realization.

Christian nonviolence does not encourage or excuse hatred of a special class, nation, or social group. It is not merely *anti*-this or that. In other words, the evangelical realism which is demanded of the Christian should make it impossible for him to generalize about "the wicked" against whom he takes up moral arms in a struggle for righteousness. He will not let himself be persuaded that the adversary is totally wicked and can therefore never be reasonable or well-intentioned, and hence need never be listened to. This attitude, which defeats the very purpose of nonviolence — openness, communication, dialogue — often accounts for the fact that some acts of civil disobedience merely antagonize the adversary without making him willing to communicate in any way whatever, except with bullets or missiles. Thomas à Becket, in Eliot's play *Murder in the Cathedral,* debated with himself, fearing that he might be seeking martyrdom merely in order to demonstrate his own righteousness and the King's injustice: "This is the greatest treason, to do the right thing for the wrong reason."

Now all these principles are fine and they accord with our Christian faith. But once we view the principles in the light of current *facts*, a practical difficulty confronts us. If the "gospel is preached to the poor," if the Christian message is essentially a message of hope and redemption for the poor, the oppressed, the underprivileged, and those who have no power humanly speaking, how are we to reconcile ourselves to the fact that Christians belong for the most part to the rich and powerful nations of the earth? Seventeen percent of the world's population control eighty percent of the world's wealth, and most of these seventeen percent are supposedly Christian. Admittedly those Christians who are interested in nonviolence are not ordinarily the wealthy ones. Nevertheless, like it or not, they share in the power and privilege of the most wealthy and mighty society the world has ever known. Even with the best subjective intentions in the world, how can they avoid a certain ambiguity in preaching nonviolence? Is this not a mystification?

We must remember Marx's accusation that "the social principles of Christianity encourage dullness, lack of self-respect, submissiveness, self-abasement, in short all the characteristics of the proletariat." We must frankly face the possibility that the nonviolence of the European or American preaching Christian meekness may conceivably be adulterated by bourgeois feelings and by an unconscious desire to preserve the status quo against violent upheaval.

On the other hand, Marx's view of Christianity is obviously tendentious and distorted. A real understanding of Christian nonviolence (backed up by the evidence of history in the Apostolic Age) shows not only that it is a *power*, but that it remains perhaps the only really effective way of transforming man and human society. After nearly fifty years of communist revolution, we find little evidence that the world is improved by violence.

Let us however seriously consider at least the *conditions* for relative honesty in the practice of Christian nonviolence.

1. Nonviolence must be aimed above all at the transformation of the present state of the world, and it must therefore be free from all occult, unconscious connivance with an unjust use of power. This poses enormous problems — for if nonviolence is too political it becomes drawn into the power struggle and identified with one side or another in that struggle, while if it is totally apolitical it runs the risk of being ineffective or at best merely symbolic.

2. The nonviolent resistance of the Christian who belongs to one of the powerful nations and who is himself in some sense a privileged member of world society will have to be clearly not *for himself* but *for others,* that is, for the poor and underprivileged. (Obviously in the case of Negroes in the United States, though they may be citizens of a privileged nation, their case is different. They are clearly entitled to wage a nonviolent struggle for their rights, but even for them this struggle should be primarily for *truth itself* — this being the source of their power.)

3. In the case of nonviolent struggle for peace — the threat of nuclear war abolishes all privileges. Under the bomb there is not much distinction between rich and poor. In fact the richest nations are usually the most threatened. Nonviolence must simply avoid the ambiguity of an unclear and *confusing protest* that hardens the warmakers in their self-righteous blindness. This means in fact that *in this case above all nonviolence must avoid a facile and fanatical self-righteousness,* and refrain from being satisfied with dramatic self-justifying gestures.

4. Perhaps the most insidious temptation to be avoided is one which is characteristic of the power structure itself: this fetishism of immediate visible results. Modern society understands "possibilities" and "results" in terms of a superficial and quantitative idea of efficacy. One of the missions of Christian nonviolence is to restore a different standard of practical judgment in social conflicts. This means that the Christian humility of nonviolent action must establish itself in the minds

and memories of modern man not only as *conceivable* and *possible,* but as *a desirable alternative* to what he now considers the only realistic possibility: namely, political technique backed by force. Here the human dignity of nonviolence must manifest itself clearly in terms of a freedom and a nobility which are able to resist political manipulation and brute force and show them up as arbitrary, barbarous, and irrational. This will not be easy. The temptation to get publicity and quick results by spectacular tricks or by forms of protest that are merely odd and provocative but whose human meaning is not clear may defeat this purpose.

The realism of nonviolence must be made evident by humility and self-restraint which clearly show frankness and open-mindedness and invite the adversary to serious and reasonable discussion.

Instead of trying to use the adversary as leverage for one's own effort to realize an ideal, nonviolence seeks only to enter into a dialogue with him in order to attain, together with him, the common good of *man.* Nonviolence must be realistic and concrete. Like ordinary political action, it is no more than the "art of the possible." But precisely the advantage of nonviolence is that it has a *more Christian and more humane notion of what is possible.* Where the powerful believe that only power is efficacious, the nonviolent resister is persuaded of the superior efficacy of love, openness, peaceful negotiation, and above all of truth. For power can guarantee the interests of *some men* but it can never foster the good of *man.* Power always protects the good of some at the expense of all the others. Only love can attain and preserve the good of all. Any claim to build the security of *all* on force is a manifest imposture.

It is here that genuine humility is of the greatest importance. Such humility, united with true Christian courage (because it is based on trust in God and not in one's own ingenuity and tenacity), is itself a way of communicating the message that one is interested only in truth and in the genuine rights of others.

Conversely, our authentic interest in the common good above all will help us to be humble, and to distrust our own hidden drive to self-assertion.

5. Christian nonviolence, therefore, is convinced that the manner in which the conflict for truth is waged will itself manifest or obscure the truth. To fight for truth by dishonest, violent, inhuman, or unreasonable means would simply betray the truth one is trying to vindicate. The absolute refusal of evil or suspect means is a necessary element in the witness of nonviolence.

As Pope Paul said before the United Nations Assembly in 1965, "Men cannot be brothers if they are not humble. No matter how justified it may appear, pride provokes tensions and struggles for prestige, domination, colonialism and egoism. In a word *pride shatters brotherhood*." He went on to say that the attempts to establish peace on the basis of violence were in fact a manifestation of human pride. "If you wish to be brothers, let the weapons fall from your hands. You cannot love with offensive weapons in your hands."

6. A test of our sincerity in the practice of nonviolence is this: Are we willing to *learn something from the adversary*? If a *new truth* is made known to us by him or through him, will we accept it? Are we willing to admit that he is not totally inhumane, wrong, unreasonable, cruel, etc.? This is important. If he sees that we are completely incapable of listening to him with an open mind, our nonviolence will have nothing to say to him except that we distrust him and seek to outwit him. Our readiness to see some good in him and to agree with some of his ideas (though tactically this might look like a weakness on our part), actually gives us power: the power of sincerity and of truth. On the other hand, if we are obviously unwilling to accept any truth that we have not first discovered and declared ourselves, we show by that very fact that we are interested not in the truth so much as in "being right." Since the adversary is presumably interested in being right also, and in proving himself right by what he considers the superior argument of force, we end up

where we started. Nonviolence has great power, provided that it really witnesses to truth and not just to self-righteousness.

The dread of being open to the ideas of others generally comes from our hidden insecurity about our own convictions. We fear that we may be "converted" — or perverted — by a pernicious doctrine. On the other hand, if we are mature and objective in our open-mindedness, we may find that viewing things from a basically different perspective — that of our adversary — we discover our own truth in a new light and are able to understand our own ideal more realistically.

Our willingness to take *an alternative approach* to a problem will perhaps relax the obsessive fixation of the adversary on his view, which we believe is the only reasonable possibility and which he is determined to impose on everyone else by coercion.

It is the refusal of alternatives — a compulsive state of mind which one might call the "ultimatum complex" — which makes wars in order to force the unconditional acceptance of one oversimplified interpretation of reality. This mission of Christian humility in social life is not merely to edify, but to *keep minds open to many alternatives*. The rigidity of a certain type of Christian thought has seriously impaired this capacity, which nonviolence must recover.

Needless to say, Christian humility must not be confused with a mere desire to win approval and to find reassurances by conciliating others superficially.

7. Christian hope and Christian humility are inseparable. The quality of nonviolence is decided largely by the purity of the Christian hope behind it. In its insistence on certain human values, the Second Vatican Council, following *Pacem in Terris,* displayed a basically optimistic trust *in man himself.* Not that there is not wickedness in the world, but today trust in God cannot be completely divorced from a certain trust in man. The Christian knows that there are radically sound possibilities in every man, and he believes that love and grace always have the power to bring out those possibilities at the most unexpected

moments. Therefore if he has hopes that God will grant peace to the world it is because he also trusts that man, God's creature, is not basically evil: that there is in man a potentiality for peace and order which can be realized provided the right conditions are there. The Christian will do his part in creating these conditions by preferring love and trust to hate and suspiciousness. Obviously, once again, this "hope in man" must not be naïve. But experience itself has shown, in the last few years, how much an attitude of simplicity and openness can do to break down barriers of suspicion that had divided men for centuries.

It is therefore very important to understand that Christian humility implies not only a certain wise reserve in regard to one's own judgments — a good sense which sees that we are not always necessarily infallible in our ideas — but it also cherishes positive and trustful expectations of others. A supposed "humility" which is simply depressed about itself and about the world is usually a false humility. This negative, self-pitying "humility" may cling desperately to dark and apocalyptic expectations, and refuse to let go of them. It is secretly convinced that only tragedy and evil can possibly come from our present world situation. This secret conviction cannot be kept hidden. It will manifest itself in our attitudes, in our social action and in our protest. It will show that in fact we despair of reasonable dialogue with anyone. It will show that we expect only the worst. Our action seeks only to block or frustrate the adversary in some way. A protest that from the start declares itself to be in despair is hardly likely to have valuable results. At best it provides an outlet for the personal frustrations of the one protesting. It enables him to articulate his despair in public. This is not the function of Christian nonviolence. This pseudo-prophetic desperation has nothing to do with the beatitudes, even the third. No blessedness has been promised to those who are merely sorry for themselves.

In resume, the meekness and humility which Christ extolled in the Sermon on the Mount and which are the basis of true

Christian nonviolence are inseparable from an eschatological Christian hope which is completely open to the presence of God in the world and therefore to the presence of our brother who is always seen, no matter who he may be, in the perspectives of the Kingdom. Despair is not permitted to the meek, the humble, the afflicted, the ones famished for justice, the merciful, the clean of heart and the peacemakers. All the beatitudes "hope against hope," bear everything, believe everything, hope for everything, endure everything" (I Corinthians 13:7). The beatitudes are simply aspects of love. They refuse to despair of the world and abandon it to a supposedly evil fate which it has brought upon itself. Instead, like Christ himself, the Christian takes upon his own shoulders the yoke of the Savior, meek and humble of heart. This yoke is the burden of the world's sin with all its confusions, and all its problems. These sins, confusions and problems are our very own. We do not disown them.

Christian nonviolence derives its hope from the promise of Christ: "Fear not, little flock, for the Father has prepared for you a Kingdom" (Luke 12:32).

The hope of the Christian must be, like the hope of a child, pure and full of trust. The child is totally available in the present because he has relatively little to remember, his experience of evil is as yet brief, and his anticipation of the future does not extend far. The Christian, in his humility and faith, must be as totally available to his brother, to his world, in the present, as the child is. But he cannot see the world with childlike innocence and simplicity unless his memory is cleared of past evils by forgiveness, and his anticipation of the future is hopefully free of craft and calculation. For this reason, the humility of Christian nonviolence is at once patient and uncalculating. The chief difference between nonviolence and violence is that the latter depends entirely on its own calculations. The former depends entirely on God and on His word.

— "Blessed Are the Meek: The Christian Roots
of Nonviolence," PP 248–58

A LETTER
TO A PEACEMAKER

During the sixties, Thomas Merton corresponded with a number of peace activists who kept him informed about developments in the peace movement. But their letters were much more than an exchange of information, as illustrated by the following excerpt from Merton's letter to Jim Forest. Forest was twenty years old and living at the Catholic Worker when he first wrote to Merton in 1961. In 1964, Forest helped to found the Catholic Peace Fellowship. In 1965, overwhelmed by the work to be done and in a "bleak mood," Forest asked Merton for "some thoughts that would help."

Do not depend on the hope of results. When you are doing the sort of work you have taken on, essentially an apostolic work, you may have to face the fact that your work will be apparently worthless and even achieve no result at all, if not perhaps results opposite to what you expect. As you get used to this idea you start more and more to concentrate not on the results but on the value, the rightness, the truth of the work itself....

You are fed up with words, and I don't blame you. I am nauseated by them sometimes. I am also, to tell the truth, nauseated with ideals and with causes. This sounds like heresy, but I think you will understand what I mean. It is so easy to get engrossed with ideas and slogans and myths that in the end one is left holding the bag, empty, with no trace of meaning left in it....

The CPF [Catholic Peace Fellowship] is not going to stop the war in Vietnam, and it is not even going to cause very many Catholics to think differently about war and peace. It is simply going to become another image among images, in the minds of most Catholics, something around which are centered some vague emotional reactions, for or against. Nevertheless, you will probably, if you continue as you do, *begin* the laborious job of

changing the national mind and opening up the national conscience. How far will you get? God alone knows. All that you
and I can ever hope for in terms of visible results is that we
will have perhaps contributed *something* to a clarification of
Christian truth in this society, and as a result a *few* people may
have got straight about some things and opened up to the grace
of God and made some sense out of their lives, helping a few
more to do the same. As for the big results, these are not in
your hands or mine, but they can suddenly happen, and we can
share in them: but there is no point in building our lives on this
personal satisfaction, which may be denied us and which after
all is not that important.

So the next step in the process is for you to see that your
own thinking about what you are doing is crucially important.
You are probably striving to build yourself an identity in your
work and your witness. You are using it so to speak to protect
yourself against nothingness, annihilation. That is not the right
use of your work. All the good that you will do will come not
from you but from the fact that you have allowed yourself, in
the obedience of faith, to be used by God's love. Think of this
more and gradually you will be free from the need to prove
yourself, and you can be more open to the power that will work
through you without your knowing it.

The great thing after all is to live, not to pour out your life
in the service of a myth: and we turn the best things into myths.
If you can get free from the domination of causes and just serve
Christ's truth, you will be able to do more and will be less
crushed by the inevitable disappointments....

The real hope, then, is not in something we think we can do,
but in God who is making something good out of it in some
way we cannot see. If we can do His will, we will be helping
in this process. But we will not necessarily know all about it
beforehand.

            —Letter to James Forest, February 21, 1965, HGL 294–97

MERTON'S PRAYER FOR PEACE

This prayer was read in the House of Representatives on April 12, 1962.

Almighty and merciful God, Father of all men, Creator and Ruler of the Universe, Lord of History, whose designs are inscrutable, whose glory is without blemish, whose compassion for the errors of men is inexhaustible, in your will is our peace.

Mercifully hear this prayer which rises to you from the tumult and desperation of a world in which you are forgotten, in which your name is not invoked, your laws are derided, and your presence is ignored. Because we do not know you, we have no peace.

From the heart of an eternal silence, you have watched the rise of empires, and seen the smoke of their downfall.

You have seen Egypt, Assyria, Babylon, Greece, and Rome, once powerful, carried away like sand in the wind.

You have witnessed the impious fury of ten thousand fratricidal wars, in which great powers have torn whole continents to shreds in the name of peace and justice.

And now our nation itself stands in imminent danger of a war the like of which has never been seen!

This nation dedicated to freedom, not to power,

Has obtained, through freedom, a power it did not desire.

And seeking by that power to defend its freedom, it is enslaved by the process and policies of power.

Must we wage a war we do not desire, a war that can do us no good,

And which our very hatred of war forces us to prepare?

A day of ominous decision has now dawned on this free nation.

Armed with a titanic weapon, and convinced of our own right,

We face a powerful adversary, armed with the same weapon, equally convinced that he is right.

In this moment of destiny, this moment we never foresaw, we
cannot afford to fail.

Our choice of peace or war may decide our judgment and
publish it in an eternal record.

In this fatal moment of choice in which we might begin the
patient architecture of peace

We may also take the last step across the rim of chaos.

Save us then from our obsessions! Open our eyes, dissipate confusions, teach us to understand ourselves and our adversary!

Let us never forget that sins against the law of love are punished
by loss of faith,

And those without faith stop at no crime to achieve their ends!

Help us to be masters of the weapons that threaten to master us.

Help us to use our science for peace and plenty, not for war
and destruction.

Show us how to use atomic power to bless our children's
children, not to blight them.

Save us from the compulsion to follow our adversaries in all
that we most hate, confirming them in their hatred and
suspicion of us.

Resolve our inner contradictions, which now grow beyond
belief and beyond bearing.

They are at once a torment and a blessing: for if you had not
left us the light of conscience, we would not have to endure
them.

Teach us to be long-suffering in anguish and insecurity.

Teach us to wait and trust.

Grant light, grant strength and patience to all who work for
peace,

To this Congress, our President, our military forces, and our
adversaries.

Grant us prudence in proportion to our power,

Wisdom in proportion to our science,

Humaneness in proportion to our wealth and might.

And bless our earnest will to help all races and people to travel,
   in friendship with us,
Along the road to justice, liberty, and lasting peace:
But grant us above all to see that our ways are not necessarily
   your ways,
That we cannot fully penetrate the mystery of your designs
And that the very storm of power now raging on this earth
Reveals your hidden will and your inscrutable decision.
Grant us to see your face in the lightning of this cosmic storm,
O God of holiness, merciful to men:
Grant us to seek peace where it is truly found!
   In your will, O God, is our peace!
                           Amen

                                        —PP 327–29

3

A Call to Unity

✠

We are already one.
But we imagine that we are not.
And what we have to recover is our original unity.
What we have to be is what we are.

—AJ 308

For Thomas Merton, unity was both a reality and a challenge. Speaking in Calcutta some weeks before he died, Merton shared an insight that was integral to his spirituality: he said we are "already one." This was something he knew experientially; it was a realization that had dawned and deepened in prayer. Awakened to his true being in God, he recognized that all are one in the hidden ground of Love that is God. And we are called to live in ways that are consistent with our original unity and to recover in our lives and relationships the unity that already is. While Merton was keenly aware of all the ways in which we are divided from one another, he recognized that the differences between us are finally superficial. Though real enough in one sense, the differences of culture, race, ethnicity, and religion are at root illusory.

In the midst of a divided world, Merton felt himself called to be an instrument of unity. "If I can understand something of myself and something of others, I can begin to share with them the work of building the foundations of spiritual unity." Though neither a professional ecumenist nor a specialist in interreligious *dialogue, Merton modeled a way of encounter and dialogue in his conversations and correspondence with Christians, Jews, Muslims, Buddhists, and Hindus. Deeply rooted in his own tradition, he was open and receptive to the wisdom of the world's religions. Merton embodied the spirit that is essential to building unity: he was open to the experience and perspective of others and respectful of their beliefs and practice. He was also clear and firm in his own faith convictions. Searching for common ground, he knew well, does not mean discounting one's own roots.*

In the initial selections in this chapter, Merton voices his own calling to unity. In subsequent selections, gathered from his writings and transcriptions of his talks, Merton reflects on the meaning of unity and how we might go about realizing it in our relationships and our world. Sharing his vision, Merton invites us to say yes to the call to realize the unity that already is.

MERTON'S OWN VOCATION TO UNITY

If I can understand something of myself and something of others, I can begin to share with them the work of building the foundations for spiritual unity. But first we must work together at dissipating the more absurd fictions which make unity impossible.

Cause to disappear, vanish, disperse,

—CGB 82

•

If I can unite *in myself* the thought and the devotion of Eastern and Western Christendom, the Greek and the Latin Fathers, the Russians with the Spanish mystics, I can prepare in myself the reunion of divided Christians. From that secret and unspoken unity in myself can eventually come a visible and manifest unity of all Christians. If we want to bring together what is divided, we can not do so by imposing one division upon the other or absorbing one division into the other. But if we do this, the

union is not Christian. It is political, and doomed to further
conflict. We must contain all divided worlds in ourselves and
transcend them in Christ.   —CGB 12

•

*"Des hommes comme Saint Seraphim, François d'Assise et bien
d'autres ont accompli dans leur vie l'union des Eglises."* ["Men
like Saint Seraphim, Saint Francis of Assisi, and many others
accomplished in their very life the union of the churches."]

This profound and simple statement of an Orthodox Metro-
politan, Eulogius, gives the key to ecumenism for monks, and
indeed for everyone.

If I do not have unity in myself, how can I even think,
let alone speak, of unity among Christians? Yet, of course, in
seeking unity for all Christians, I also attain unity within myself.

The heresy of individualism: thinking oneself a completely
self-sufficient unit and asserting this imaginary "unity" against
all others. The affirmation of the self as simply "not the other."
But when you seek to affirm your unity by denying that you
have anything to do with anyone else, by negating everyone else
in the universe until you come down to *you*: what is there left
to affirm? Even if there were something to affirm, you would
have no breath left with which to affirm it.

The true way is just the opposite: the more I am able to affirm others, to say "yes" to them in myself, by discovering them
in myself and myself in them, the more real I am. I am fully real
if my own heart says *yes* to *everyone*.

I will be a better Catholic, not if I can *refute* every shade
of Protestantism, but if I can affirm the truth in it and still go
further.

So, too, with the Muslims, the Hindus, the Buddhists, etc.
This does not mean syncretism, indifferentism, the vapid and
careless friendliness that accepts everything by thinking of nothing. There is much that one cannot "affirm" and "accept," but
first one must say "yes" where one really can.

If I affirm myself as a Catholic merely by denying all that is
Muslim, Jewish, Protestant, Hindu, Buddhist, etc., in the end I
will find that there is not much left for me to affirm as a Catholic: and certainly no breath of the Spirit with which to affirm it.
—CGB 128–29

•

I cannot be a Catholic unless it is made quite clear to the world
that I am a Jew and a Moslem, unless I am execrated as a
Buddhist and denounced for having undermined all that this
comfortable and social Catholicism stands for: this lining up of
cassocks, this regimenting of birettas. I throw my birettas in the
river. (But I don't have one.)
—Letter to Czeslaw Milosz, January 18, 1962, CT 79

•

To be truly Catholic is not merely to be correct according to
an abstractly universal standard of truth, but also and above
all to be able to enter into the problems and the joys of all, to
understand all, to be all things to all men.   —CGB 167

•

For myself, I am more and more convinced that my job is to
clarify something of the tradition that lives in me, and in which
I live: the tradition of wisdom and spirit that is found not only
in Western Christendom but in Orthodoxy, and also, at least
analogously, in Asia and in Islam. Man's sanity and balance and
peace depend, I think, on his keeping alive a continuous sense
of what has been valid in his past.   —CGB 176

•

In his preface to The Complete Works of Thomas Merton,
*published in Argentina in 1958, Merton links his call to the
contemplative life with his discovery of himself as a man of*

the whole Western Hemisphere. In this piece, he not only re-
flects his passionate love for Latin America and its people but
also expresses a vision of humanity and faith that transcends the
boundaries of geography and culture.

I am one of millions whose destiny brought him from the shores
of Europe to become a citizen of the Western Hemisphere, a
man of the New World. I actually already belonged to the New
World in a sense since my mother's family had lived there for
several generations. I came seeking an answer to the inscrutable
problems of life and found an answer both old and new — an
answer pertaining to no time, country, continent, or culture. I
found the word of salvation in the New World. I also found a
paradoxical vocation for the contemplative life — a vocation in-
comprehensible to some, as if the contemplative life is confined
to the Old World which is dying rather than to the New World
which is being born....

The contemplative life applies wherever there is life. Wherever man and society exist; where there are hopes, ideals,
aspirations for a better future; where there is love — and where
there is mingled pain and happiness — there the contemplative
life has a place, because life, happiness, pain, ideals, aspirations, work, art, and other things have significance. If these
things have no significance, why waste our time on them? But,
if they have significance, then the independent significance of
each must converge in some way into a central and universal
significance which comes from a hidden reality. This central
reality has to be a "catholic" reality, a "divine" reality. The
reality central to my life is the life of God. To know this is the
contemplative's objective.

In my case, the word of salvation, the gospel of Jesus Christ,
has led me to solitude and to silence. My vocation is rare perhaps, but contemplation does not exist only within the walls
of the cloister. Every man, to live a life full of significance, is
called simply to know the significant interior of life and to find

ultimate significance in its proper inscrutable existence, in spite of himself, in spite of the world and appearances, in the Living God. Every man born on this earth is called to find and realize himself in Christ and, through Him, to comprehend the unity of Christ with all men, so much so that he loves them as they love themselves and is one with them almost as he is one with himself: then the spirit of Christ is one with those who love Him.

In the silence of the countryside and the forest, in the cloistered solitude of my monastery, I have discovered the whole Western Hemisphere. Here I have been able, through the grace of God, to explore the New World, without traveling from city to city, without flying over the Andes or the Amazon, stopping one day here, two there, and then continuing on. Perhaps if I had traveled in this manner, I should have seen nothing: generally those who travel most see the least.

It seems that I have heard the voice of all the hemisphere in the silence of my monastery, a voice that speaks from the depths of my being with a clarity at once magnificent and terrible: as if I had in my heart the vast and solitary pampas, the brilliant hoarfrost of the Bolivian plateau, the thin air of the terraced valleys of the Incas, the splendor and suavity of Quito, the cold plains of Bogotá, and the mysterious jungles of the Amazon. It seems that entire cities with great opulence and terrible indigence side by side live inside me. It seems that the ancient civilizations of Mexico, older even than Egypt, gather in unspeakable silence in my heart. It seems that I hear in the even more profound silence of Peru the forgotten syllables of ancient wisdom which has never died and which contains in its secrets an image of truth that no man has recognized, an image, symbolic and prophetic, like that of Jesus Christ. It seems that the unending beauty of the New World with its limitless possibilities moves within me like a giant sleeper in whose presence I am unable to remain indifferent. In reality, it seems at times that this presence inside me speaks with the voice of God Himself;

and I struggle vainly to grasp and to understand some word, some syllable of the destiny of the New World — the destiny that is still hidden in the mystery of Providence.

One thing I know — that it is my destiny to be a contemplative, a Christian, and an American. I can satisfy my vocation with nothing that is partial or provincial. I cannot be a "North American" who knows only the rivers, the plains, the mountains, and the cities of the north, the north where there are few Indians, where the land was colonized and cultivated by the Puritans, where, under the audacious and sarcastic splendor of the skyscrapers, one rarely sees the Cross and where the Holy Virgin, when she is represented at all, is pale and melancholy and carries no child in her arms. This north is grand, powerful, rich, intelligent; it has a warmth of its own, a surprising humility, a charity, an inner purity which the stranger does not know. But it is incomplete. It is neither the better nor the richer part of the hemisphere. It is perhaps, at this point in time, the most important region of the world, but it is, nonetheless, not sufficient in itself and it lacks fundamental roots. It lacks the roots of the old America, the America of Mexico and the Andes, where silent and contemplative Asians came, millenniums ago, to construct their hieratic cities. It lacks the intense fervor and fecundity of Brazil, which is also African, which smiles with the grin of the Congo and laughs with the childlike innocence of Portugal. The northern half of this New World lacks the force, the refinement, the prodigality of Argentina with all the lyricism of its tormented and generous heart.

I cannot be a partial American and I cannot be, which is even sadder, a partial Catholic. For me Catholicism is not confined to one culture, one nation, one age, one race. My faith is not a mixture of the Irish Catholicism of the United States and the splendid and vital Catholicism, reborn during the past war, of my native France. Though I admire the cathedrals and the past of Catholicism in Latin America, my Catholicism goes beyond the Spanish tradition. I cannot believe that Catholicism is tied to the destinies of any group which confusedly expresses the economic illusions of a social class.... My Catholicism is all the world and all ages. It dates from the beginning of the world. The first man was the image of Christ and contained Christ, even as he was created, as savior in his heart. The first man was destined to be the ancestor of his Redeemer and the first woman was the mother of all life, in the image of the Immaculate Daughter who was full of grace, Mother of mercy, Mother of the saved....

Contemplation cannot construct a new world by itself. Contemplation does not feed the hungry; it does not clothe the naked; it does not teach the ignorant; and it does not return the sinner to peace, truth, and union with God. But without contemplation we cannot see what we do in our apostolate. Without contemplation we cannot understand the significance of the world in which we must act. Without contemplation we remain small, limited, divided, partial: we adhere to the insufficient, permanently united to our narrow group and its interests, losing sight of justice and charity, seized by the passions of the moment, and, finally, we betray Christ. Without contemplation, without the intimate, silent, secret pursuit of truth through love, our action loses itself in the world and becomes dangerous. Yet, if our contemplation is fanatic or false, our action becomes much more dangerous. We should lose ourselves to win the world; we should humble ourselves to find Christ everywhere and to love Him in all beings: instead, we betray Him by not seeing Him in those whom we harm unconsciously while we "innocently" pray for them....

This, then, is what seems to me so important about America — and the great function of my vocation in it: to know America in its totality, to be a complete American, a man of the whole hemisphere, of the whole New World; to be a complete Christian, a complete contemplative, and through this, to help others to know Christ in the fullness of maturity, in all His universality, until we all attain to the unity of faith and of the deep knowledge of the Son of God, to perfect manhood, to the mature measure of the fullness of Christ; and this He has done that we may be now no longer children, tossed to and fro and carried about by every wind of doctrine devised in the wickedness of men, in craftiness, according to the wiles of error; rather are we to practice the truth in love, and so to grow up in all things in Him who is the head, Christ. (Ephesians 4:13–15)

...We must work together as Americans and Christians, as brothers and as builders — I with my books and prayers, you with your work and prayers. Separately we are incomplete. Together we are strong with the strength of God. Oh, my brothers and sisters of the South...we are already one in our love of truth, our passion for freedom, and our adoration of the Living God.

— "Preface to the Argentine Edition of
The Complete Works of Thomas Merton," HR 39–44

KEEPING FAITH

Keeping faith was for Merton a matter of balancing faithfulness to tradition with openness to the signs of the times. He challenged "rigid, stereotyped, bourgeois notions" and "mere external conformity" and hoped that he was what Pope John XXIII was: "a progressive with a deep respect and love for tradition."

Christian missionaries in South America came with their eyes closed by pride, unable to see Christ in those whom they "discovered" and seeking only to impose their own beliefs, which meant their own "culture." Thus they did and did not preach the Gospel. They were and were not true to Christ. This awful ambiguity has been the tragedy of Christianity since the Middle Ages. It has been part of the rise and decline of the West, and contributed fatally to the terrible split in the world.

...The world is lying inert under a huge weight of spiritual torpor and heaviness, with conscience gone dead and all awareness extinct. And the disaster hangs over all men. This is indeed the time for purity of heart, compunction and detachment, to embrace the truth....

You must understand by now that I do not entertain formally conventional notions of the Church. I certainly believe with all my heart in the Church, none more so. But I absolutely refuse to take the rigid, stereotyped, bourgeois notions that are acceptable to most Catholics and which manage in the long run to veil the true mystery of Christ and make it utterly unattainable to some people. You can pull my leg all you want, it stretches indefinitely, and we both understand quite well the way in which you belong to Christ. We both belong to Him in His mercy, which is inscrutable and infinite and reaches into the inmost depths of every being, but especially of all who, with all their deficiencies and limitations, seek only truth and love, as best they can. I do not understand too much of any kind of Church which is made up entirely of people whose external conformity has made them comfortable and secure, and has given them the privilege of looking down on everybody else who is automatically "wrong" because not conformed to them. This does not seem to me to have a great deal to do with the message of Christ. The Church is indeed visible, yes, but it depends what you mean by "visible." Not Cadillacs, surely.

> — Letter to Dona Louisa Coomaraswamy,
> September 24, 1961, HGL 132–33

•

One of the great problems after this Council is certainly going to be the division between progressives and conservatives, and this may prove to be rather ugly in some cases, though it may also be a fruitful source of sacrifice for those who are determined to seek the will of God and not their own. I do not speak here of bishops, but of ordinary priests, theologians, lay people, and all who voice their opinions one way or another.

For my own part I consider myself neither conservative nor an extreme progressive. I would like to think I am what Pope John was — a progressive with a deep respect and love for tradition — in other words a progressive who wants to preserve a very clear and marked *continuity* with the past and not make silly and idealistic compromises with the present — yet to be *completely open* to the modern world while retaining the clearly defined, traditionally Catholic position.

The extreme progressives seem to me, as far as I can judge with the poverty of my information, to be hasty, irresponsible, in many ways quite frivolous in their exaggerated and confused enthusiasms. They also seem to me at times to be fanatically incoherent, but I do not sense in them the chilling malice and meanness which comes through in some of the utterances of extreme conservatives.

The thing that disquiets me most is the fact that the progressives, though perhaps a majority, do not seem to have the dogged and concerted stamina of the conservatives. The extreme conservatives seem to me to be people who feel themselves so menaced that they will go to *any length* in order to defend their own fanatical concept of the Church. This concept seems to me to be not only static and inert, but in complete continuity with what is most questionable and indeed scandalous in the history of the Church: Inquisition, persecution, intolerance, Papal power, clerical influence, alliance with worldly power, love of wealth and pomp, etc. This is a picture of the Church which has become a scandal and these people are intent on preserving the scandal at the cost of greater scandal.

To begin with, while they are always the ones who make the shrillest noises about authority and obedience, they seem to be shockingly unready to practice the most elementary obedience or to display the most rudimentary faith that the Council is guided by the Holy Spirit as soon as something is decided which they do not approve. They are so convinced that *they* are the Church that they are almost ready to declare the majority of bishops to be virtual apostates, rather than obey the Council and the Pope. At the same time, of course, their hysteria suggests that they are having a little trouble handling the guilt which this inevitably arouses in them.

On the other hand, the refusal of the extreme progressives to pay any attention to *any* traditional teaching which would give them a common basis for rational discussion with conservatives is surely scandalous also — especially when it is allied with an arrogant triumphalism of its own, and when it simply ridicules all opposition. This is not only foolish, but seems to show a serious lack of that love to which they frequently appeal in justification of their procedures. Though they are continually shouting about "openness" one finds them hermetically closed to their fellow Catholics and to the Church's own past, and there is some validity to the conservative accusation that these extreme progressives often are more open to Marxism, to positivism, or to existentialism than they are to what is generally recognizable as Catholic truth.

It has been remarked with truth that conservatives and progressives in the Church are so concerned with total victory over each other that they are more and more closed to each other. If this is the case, one seriously wonders about the value and significance of the much touted "openness" to non-Catholics. An ecumenism that does not begin with charity *within* one's own Church remains questionable.   — CGB 285–87

•

In September 1961, Merton wrote to Nicaraguan journalist Pablo Antonio Cuadra that he had completed a "long letter" for publication, entitled "A Letter to Pablo Antonio Cuadra concerning Giants." Merton explained that the giants were "the big

*power blocs that are beginning to enter the final stages of the
death struggle in which they will tear themselves to pieces." He
labeled the Soviet Union, Gog and the United Sates, Magog.
"Gog is the lover of power, Magog is absorbed in the cult of
money: their idols differ...but their madness is the same." Merton included the "letter," which had already been published in
Nicaragua, Argentina, San Salvador, and England, in a collection
of poetry entitled* Emblems in a Season of Fury.

Let me be quite succinct: the greatest sin of the European-
Russian-American complex which we call "the West" (and this
sin has spread its own way to China), is not only greed and
cruelty, not only moral dishonesty and infidelity to truth, but
above all *its unmitigated arrogance towards the rest of the
human race.* Western civilization is now in full decline into barbarism (a barbarism that springs *from within itself*) because it
has been guilty of a twofold disloyalty: to God and to Man.
To a Christian who believes in the mystery of the Incarnation,
and who by that belief means something more than a pious
theory without real humanistic implications, this is not two dis-
loyalties but one. Since the Word was made Flesh, God is in
man. God is in *all men.* All men are to be seen and treated
as Christ. Failure to do this, the Lord tells us, involves con-
demnation for disloyalty to the most fundamental of revealed
truths. "I was thirsty and you gave me not to drink. I was hungry and you gave me not to eat..." (Matthew 25:42). This
could be extended in every possible sense: and is meant to
be so extended, all over the entire area of human needs, not
only for bread, for work, for liberty, for health, but also for
truth, for belief, for love, for acceptance, for fellowship and
understanding.

One of the great tragedies of the Christian West is the fact
that for all the good will of the missionaries and colonizers (they
certainly meant well, and behaved humanly, according to their
lights which were somewhat brighter than ours), they could not

recognize that *the races they conquered were essentially equal to themselves and in some ways superior.*

It was certainly right that Christian Europe should bring Christ to the Indians of Mexico and the Andes, as well as to the Hindus and the Chinese: but where they failed was in their inability to *encounter Christ* already potentially present in the Indians, the Hindus, and the Chinese. . . .

It is my belief that we should not be too sure of having found Christ in ourselves until we have found him also in the part of humanity that is most remote from our own.

Christ is found not in loud and pompous declarations but in humble and fraternal dialogue. He is found less in a truth that is imposed than in a truth that is shared.

If I insist on giving you my truth, and never stop to receive your truth in return, then there can be no truth between us. Christ is present "where two or three are gathered in my name." But to be gathered in the name of Christ is to be gathered in the name of the Word made flesh, of God made man. It is therefore to be gathered in the faith that God has become man and can be seen in man, that he can speak in man and that he can enlighten and inspire love in and through any man I meet. It is true that the visible Church alone has the official mission to sanctify and teach all nations, but no man knows that the stranger he meets coming out of the forest in a new country is not already an invisible member of Christ and perhaps one who has some providential or prophetic message to utter.

Whatever India may have had to say to the West she was forced to remain silent. Whatever China had to say, though some of the first missionaries heard it and understood it, the message was generally ignored as irrelevant. Did anyone pay attention to the voices of the Maya and the Inca, who had deep things to say? By and large their witness was merely suppressed. No one considered that the children of the Sun might, after all, hold in their hearts a spiritual secret. On the contrary, abstract discussions were engaged in to determine whether, in terms of academic philosophy, the Indian was to be considered a rational animal. One shudders at the voice of cerebral Western arrogance even then eviscerated by the rationalism that is ours today, judging the living spiritual mystery of primitive man and condemning it to exclusion from the category on which love, friendship, respect, and communion were made to depend.

God speaks, and God is to be heard, not only on Sinai, not only in my own heart, but in the *voice of the stranger*. That is why the peoples of the Orient, and all primitive peoples in general, make so much of the mystery of hospitality.

God must be allowed the right to speak unpredictably. The Holy Spirit, the very voice of Divine Liberty, must always be like the wind in "blowing where he pleases" (John 3:8). In the mystery of the Old Testament there was already a tension between the Law and the Prophets. In the New Testament the Spirit himself is Law, and he is everywhere. He certainly inspires and protects the visible Church, but if we cannot see him unexpectedly in the stranger and the alien, we will not understand him even in the Church. We must find him in our enemy, or we may lose him even in our friend. We must find him in the pagan, or we will lose him in our own selves, substituting for his living presence an empty abstraction. How can we reveal to others what we cannot discover in them ourselves? We must, then, see the truth in the stranger, and the truth we see must be a newly living truth, not just a projection of a dead conventional idea of our own — a projection of our own self upon the stranger.

The desecration, de-sacralization of the modern world is manifest above all by the fact that the stranger is of no account. As soon as he is "displaced" he is completely unacceptable. He fits into no familiar category, he is unexplained and therefore a threat to complacency. Everything not easy to account for must be wiped out, and mystery must be wiped out with it. An alien presence interferes with the superficial and faked clarity of our own rationalizations....

If only North Americans had realized, after a hundred and

fifty years, that Latin Americans really existed. That they were really people. That they spoke a different language. That they had a culture. That they had more than something to sell! Money has totally corrupted the brotherhood that should have united all the peoples of America. It has destroyed the sense of relationship, the spiritual community that had already begun to flourish in the years of Bolivar. But no! Most North Americans still don't know, and don't care, that Brazil speaks a language other than Spanish, that all Latin Americans do not live for the siesta, that all do not spend their days and nights playing the guitar and making love. They have never awakened to the fact that Latin America is by and large culturally superior to the United States, not only on the level of the wealthy minority which has absorbed more of the sophistication of Europe, but also among the desperately poor indigenous cultures, some of which are rooted in a past that has never yet been surpassed on this continent.

So the tourist drinks tequila, and thinks it is no good, and waits for the fiesta he has been told to wait for. How should he realize that the Indian who walks down the street with half a house on his head and a hole in his pants is Christ? All the tourist thinks is that it is odd for so many Indians to be called Jesus.   — "A Letter to Pablo Antonio Cuadra concerning Giants," CP 380–88

•

In his essay commemorating the 150th Anniversary of the Founding of the Congregation of the Sisters of Loretto at the Foot of the Cross (1812–1962), Merton contrasts "false unity," which is the "work of force," with "true unity," which is the "work of love." Keeping faith necessitates the latter.

There is nothing more positive, more creative than the faith by which the Creator of all dwells and acts in our hearts. And yet, as we know from our own past history, the ideal of "keeping the faith" can sometimes dwindle into something very negative, resentful, and obtuse: a mere "no" to everything that we do not agree with. We can no longer afford to barricade ourselves in our Catholic environment and regard it as a little smug fortress of security in a world of pagans. Now most of all we are obliged by our faith and by our love of truth to commit ourselves humbly and completely not only to the message of Christ but also to all that is valid in human culture and civilization: for this too is His by right. Not only is it something that we must salvage for Him, but more, it is not unconnected with our own salvation. If the Lord of all took flesh and sanctified all nature, restoring it to the Father by His resurrection, we too have our work to do in extending the power of the resurrection to the whole world of our time by our prayer, our thought, our work and our whole life. Nothing so effectively prevents this as the division, the discontinuity of spiritual lives that place God and prayer in one compartment, work and apostolate in another, as if prayer and work were somehow opposed. The Cross is the sign of contradiction, but also and above all the sign of reconciliation. It reminds us of the contradictions within ourselves, and within our society, only in order to resolve them all in unity in love of the Savior. Unity is the sign of strength and spiritual health. This unity in Christ is the true secret of our Christian and religious vocations, whether our lives be active or contemplative.

False unity is the work of force. It is violently imposed on divided entities which stubbornly refuse to be one. True unity is the work of love. It is the free union of beings that spontaneously seek to be one in the truth, preserving and elevating their separate selves by self-transcendence. False unity strives to assert itself by the denial of obstacles. True unity admits the presence of obstacles, and of divisions, in order to overcome both by humility and sacrifice.

Here, in facing contradiction, we can hope for grace from God that will produce a unity and a peace "which the world cannot give."   —LG

ONE BODY

Thomas Merton characterized No Man Is an Island *(1955) as a sequel to* Seeds of Contemplation *(1949) which developed some of what* Seeds *had taken for granted.* No Man Is an Island *"treats of some of the basic virtues on which the spiritual life depends." John Donne provided Merton with an organizing metaphor and a title that has helped to make the book a popular seller.*

Man is divided against himself and against God by his own selfishness, which divides him against his brother. This division cannot be healed by a love that places itself only on one side of the rift. Love must reach over to both sides and draw them together. We cannot love ourselves unless we love others, and we cannot love others unless we love ourselves. But a selfish love of ourselves makes us incapable of loving others. The difficulty of this commandment lies in the paradox that it would have us love ourselves unselfishly, because even our love of ourselves is something we owe to others.

This truth never becomes clear as long as we assume that each one of us, individually, is the center of the universe. We do not exist for ourselves alone, and it is only when we are fully convinced of this fact that we begin to love ourselves properly and thus also love others. . . .

Only when we see ourselves in our true human context, as members of a race which is intended to be one organism and "one body," will we begin to understand the positive importance not only of the successes but of the failures and accidents in our lives. My successes are not my own. The way to them was prepared by others. The fruit of my labors is not my own: for I am preparing the way for the achievements of another. Nor are my failures my own. They may spring from the failure of another, but they are also compensated for by another's achievement. Therefore the meaning of my life is not to be looked for merely in the sum total of my own achievements. It is seen only in the complete integration of my achievements and failures with the achievements and failures of my own generation, and society, and time. It is seen, above all, in my integration in the mystery of Christ. That was what the poet John Donne realized during a serious illness when he heard the death knell tolling for another. "The Church is Catholic, universal," he said, "so are all her actions, all that she does belongs to all. . . . Who bends not his ear to any bell which upon any occasion rings? but who can remove it from that bell which is passing a piece of himself out of this world?"

Every other man is a piece of myself, for I am a part and a member of mankind. Every Christian is part of my own body, because we are members of Christ. What I do is also done for them and with them and by them. What they do is done in me and by me and for me. But each one of us remains responsible for his own share in the life of the whole body. Charity cannot be what it is supposed to be as long as I do not see that my life represents my own allotment in the life of a whole super-natural organism to which I belong. Only when this truth is absolutely central do other doctrines fit into their proper context. Solitude, humility, self-denial, action and contemplation, the sacraments, the monastic life, the family, war and peace — none of these make sense except in relation to the central reality which is God's love living and acting in those whom He has incorporated in His Christ. Nothing at all makes sense, unless we admit, with John Donne, that: "No man is an island, entire of itself; every man is a piece of the continent, a part of the main."

—NMII xx–xxiii

AT ONE IN SPIRIT

The ground of human unity, Merton wrote to Amiya Chakravarty, is "the hidden ground of Love." At the time, Chakravarty was teaching at Smith College, where he organized an evening of

Merton readings for his students — one of whom was Diana Eck, now a professor of religion at Harvard University who recently directed On Common Ground, *a study of religious pluralism in the United States.*

It is not easy to try to say what I know I cannot say. I do really have the feeling that you have all understood and shared quite perfectly. That you have seen something that I see to be most precious — and most available too. The reality that is present to us and in us: call it Being, call it Atman, call it Pneuma ... or Silence. And the simple fact that by being attentive, by learning to listen (or recovering the natural capacity to listen which cannot be learned any more than breathing), we can find ourself engulfed in such happiness that it cannot be explained: the happiness of being at one with everything in that hidden ground of Love for which there can be no explanations.

— Letter to Amiya Chakravarty, April 13, 1967, HGL 115

•

The following is excerpted from the adaptation of a transcript of a conference Merton gave to a group of sisters in Alaska in September 1968. The excerpt captures Merton's speaking approach and style. Merton builds on ideas from the work of psychoanalyst Reza Arasteh and Jewish theologian and philosopher Martin Buber. While in Alaska, Merton was keeping an eye out for possible sites for a hermitage — a site more remote and private than that of his hermitage at Gethsemani.

Sit down and think: How would I define the real aim of my life — what would be the one word that I would choose? I suspect that everybody would say "love" or "union with God." One of the oldest and most traditional expressions is the word "unity." The contemplative life and the monastic life "unify," both in terms of community — a unity of persons in a community — and also unity within myself, the unification and the simplification of my whole personal being and the unification of all my heart and strivings in the one thing that is necessary, and that is the love of God....

My Persian friend [Dr. Reza Arasteh] wrote a book on psychoanalysis which begins with the idea that we should try to understand it in terms of man's highest development. Instead of orienting psychoanalysis to getting people out of trouble and getting them lined up with the rest of society, what we should really be doing is leading people to the highest perfection. Then he goes into the Sufist mysticism and its purpose — he calls it final integration — a final unification in which the person becomes fully and completely himself as he is intended to be, which is to say, a full and complete lover. Sufism is very strong on love of God, and the Sufi mystics are full of beautiful and lyrical songs of love for God and union of the soul with God. When this author speaks of final integration he says that real maturity is for a person to become a mystic. This is what man is made for....

I want to bring to your attention this book of Martin Buber's, *The Way of Man*, in which Buber takes stories from the Jewish mystics and develops them very simply. This particular story goes something like this: A disciple of a Jewish mystic wants to fast and he decides not to eat or drink anything for a week. He goes through six days and on the last day, tormented with thirst, he almost gives in and goes to the spring to take a drink. But he overcomes the temptation and turns back. As he leaves the spring he feels proud of overcoming himself, so he says, "Perhaps it would be better if I took a drink — then I would not be proud." He turns around, goes back to the spring and just when he is about to drink, he notices that he is no longer thirsty, so he says, "Why take a drink?" The next day he goes to see his Master and tells him triumphantly that he fasted for a whole week, and the Master, who has supernaturally seen all that took place, looks at him and says, "Patchwork!" In other words, you didn't do a good job at all.

Buber in commenting says, "Well, maybe that was not fair. After all, he did fast for a week; he yielded to human weakness a little bit, but he overcame himself." But the point Buber goes on to make is interesting and useful — most of our work is patchwork. It gets done finally, but it is put together in bits and pieces and that is not final integration. While we still act in this way, we are not really fully developed. We are not fully grown in the spiritual life if we have to shilly-shally back and forth. The fully integrated man should work in one piece, not patchwork, and Buber says that we can be unified beyond this stage. Too often we are content with patchwork; we get by with it — good! And if we do, all right, so much the better. Thank God for it. But there is more than that. We can do a better job; we can become totally unified; we are not helpless even though too often we get the feeling that the best we can do is muddle through. . . .

If we really want to be saints in the full sense of the word, we must let God's power really work on us, and build us into one piece. But we don't do that; we evade it one way or another, and this kind of evasion is almost universally accepted. If you are getting by, fine, you are not sinning so you must be virtuous; be glad of that. No, it *is* possible and we know in our hearts that it should be possible and want it to be possible, but it is by the Divine power, not by our own power. We are afraid to believe that this power is in us. But if we do admit that this Divine force is present in our souls, it is not that we will automatically be asked to do something inhumanly difficult. It is just that we have to transcend ourselves — we will have to go beyond our present level. Too often we are content to maintain a fairly decent level and never surpass it. But our life demands breakthroughs; not every day, not every week, not every month, but once in a while we must break through and go beyond where we are. You have to build up all you have done and push through with it, and then you find that you are out of the woods in a new clearing, you are somewhere else developing a new way.

Here is the point, and this is very important for everybody.
This unification is necessary and God pushes us into it when
He is going to ask us to do something unusual. Buber says that
this unification must be accomplished before a man undertakes
some unusual work. Only with a united soul will he be able so
to do it that it becomes not patchwork but all of a piece. We
get into trouble so often by finding ourselves thrown into something big that has to be patchwork because we are not ready
for it; but on the other hand when the whole thing is in God's
hand, He works all the elements together. . . .

Buber adds that people make the mistake of thinking that
unification can be achieved by asceticism, and it cannot. Simply
making a resolution to do something difficult and then doing it
does not protect the soul from its own contradictions. There is
something much deeper than that. There is something that God
has to bring about, and we can't trust in asceticism to do it. He
adds another point: this unification is never final — it is always
partial. There is always a little more unification to be achieved.
Each time we do something with a united soul, we develop a
little further. It is a sort of capital, money in the bank, so to
speak, for the future. Next time we can do things better. Buber
says that any work that I do with a united soul reacts upon
my soul, acts in the direction of new and greater unification
and leads me to a steadier unity. Thus man ultimately reaches a
point where he can rely upon his soul, where he can trust, act
with confidence.

That, I think, is something which we should all keep in mind.
And this is what we lose when we are overburdened. There are
so many little things to be done, there is such confusion, that
you get lost in it, but on the other hand, the power of God is
there. His power is in the depths of our soul and we are stronger
than we think, not because we are strong, but because God is
strong in us. We have to believe that. When Buber says unification of the soul, remember that the word "soul" is a special
kind of word; it does not just mean the soul as the form of the

body. When he talks of soul, he means the whole man — a real man. A person is real when he is a soul.

Sufism, incidentally, has some interesting things to say about who and what man is and about anthropology. Sufism divides man up in terms of his knowledge of God, his faculty for knowing God. For example, Sufism looks at man as a heart and a spirit and as a secret, and the secret is the deepest part. The secret of man is God's secret; therefore, it is in God. My secret is God's innermost knowledge of me, which He alone possesses. It is God's secret knowledge of myself in Him, which is a beautiful concept. The heart is the faculty by which man knows God and therefore Sufism develops the heart.

For us, the education of a monastic person is the education of the heart. The novitiate formation should be the formation of the heart to know God. This is a very important concept in the contemplative life, both in Sufism and in the Christian tradition. To develop a heart that knows God, not just a heart that loves God, but a heart that knows God. How does one know God in the heart? By praying in the heart. The Sufis have ways of learning to pray so that you are really praying in the heart, from the heart, not just saying words, not just thinking good thoughts or making intentions or acts of the will, but from the heart. This is a very ancient Biblical concept that is carried over from Jewish thought into monasticism. It is the spirit which loves God, in Sufism. The spirit is almost the same word as the Biblical word "spirit" — the breath of life. So man knows God with his heart, but loves God with his life. It is your living self that is an act of constant love for God and this inmost secret of man is that by which he contemplates God, it is the secret of man in God himself....

The Sufis have this beautiful development of what this secret really is: it is the word "yes" or the act of "yes." It is the secret affirmation which God places in my heart, a "yes" to Him. And that is God's secret. He knows my "yes" even when I am not saying it. My destiny in life — my final integration — is to uncover this "yes" so that my life is totally and completely a "yes" to God, a complete assent to God. When you see the contemplative life and the monastic life in that sense, you can see how they work together. The monastic life is the setting in which by obedience, poverty, the Rule, prayer, we are set up for constantly saying "yes," but the contemplative life is the inner "yes" itself. It is the real personal response, and I think that brings the two elements perfectly together.

Here is one more quotation from one of the ascetic rabbis of the seventeenth century: "No matter how low you may have fallen in your esteem, bear in mind that if you delve deeply into yourself you will discover holiness there. A holy spark resides there which, through repentance, you may fan into a consuming flame, which will burn away the dross of unholiness and unworthiness." That spark of holiness is the "yes" which, according to this view, cannot be extinguished. And this is also the Christian view. Deep in our hearts is the most profound meaning of our personality, which is that we say "yes" to God, and the spark is always there. All we need to do is to turn towards it and let it become a flame. This is the way we are made, and the monastic life and the contemplative life should be built on this religious conception of man which you do not find in ordinary psychology. (Though some of the psychologists are now moving towards it and adopting it, saying that this is the real point, although for them it is metaphor, poetry.) There are almost infinite potentialities in this concept and we must realize that what we are here for is to develop them. There is so much in us that can be brought out if we let God do it. *wow*

If someone is living in an unconditional "yes" to God's love, he or she is fully living what they came to religion for. Nothing else really matters once that is taken care of. Everybody can do this — people not in religious life, too — it is simply the Christian way of life.

— "The Life That Unifies" (adaptation of transcript of talk given to sisters in Alaska, 1968), TMA 145–55

•

Drawing from Reza Arasteh's Final Integration in the Adult Personality *(Leiden: E. J. Brill, 1965), Merton offers this description of final integration and the integrated person.*

Final integration is a state of transcultural maturity far beyond mere social adjustment, which always implies partiality and compromise. The man who is "fully born" has an entirely "inner experience of life." He apprehends his life fully and wholly from an inner ground that is at once more universal than the empirical ego and yet entirely his own. He is in a certain sense "cosmic" and "universal man." He has attained a deeper, fuller identity than that of his limited ego-self which is only a fragment of his being. He is in a certain sense identified with everybody: or in the familiar language of the New Testament...he is "all things to all men." He is able to experience their joys and sufferings as his own, without however becoming dominated by them. He has attained to a deep inner freedom — the Freedom of the Spirit we read of in the New Testament. He is guided not just by will and reason, but by: "spontaneous behavior subject to dynamic insight."...

Again, the state of insight which is final integration implies an openness, an "emptiness," a "poverty" similar to those described in such detail not only by the Rhenish mystics, by St. John of the Cross, by the early Franciscans, but also by the Sufis, the early Taoist masters and Zen Buddhists. Final integration implies the void, poverty, and nonaction which leave one entirely docile to the "Spirit" and hence a potential instrument for unusual creativity.

The man who has attained final integration is no longer limited by the culture in which he has grown up. "He has embraced *all of life.*... He has experienced qualities of every type of life": ordinary human existence, intellectual life, artistic creation, human love, religious life. He passes beyond all these limiting forms, while retaining all that is best and most universal in them, "finally giving birth to a fully comprehensive self." He accepts not only his own community, his own society, his own friends, his own culture, but all mankind. He does not remain bound to one limited set of values in such a way that he opposes them aggressively or defensively to others. He is fully "Catholic" in the best sense of the word. He has a unified vision and experience of the one truth shining out in all its various manifestations, some clearer than others, some more definite and more certain than others. He does not set these partial views up in opposition to each other, but unifies them in a dialectic or an insight of complementarity. With this view of life he is able to bring perspective, liberty, spontaneity into the lives of others. The finally integrated man is a peacemaker, and that is why there is such a desperate need for our leaders to become such men of insight....

Dr. Arasteh describes the breakthrough into final integration, in the language of Sufism. The consecrated term in Sufism is *Fana,* annihilation or disintegration, a loss of self, a real spiritual death....

For a Christian, a transcultural integration is eschatological. The rebirth of man and of society on a transcultural level is a rebirth into the transformed and redeemed time, the time of the Kingdom, the time of the Spirit, the time of "the end." It means a disintegration of the social and cultural self, the product of merely human history, and the reintegration of that self in Christ, in salvation history, in the mystery of redemption, in the Pentecostal "new creation." But this means entering into the full mystery of the eschatological Church....

The path to final integration for the individual, and for the community lies, in any case, beyond the dictates and programs of any culture ("Christian culture" included).

— "Final Integration: Toward a Monastic Therapy,"
CWA 225–31

GENUINE ECUMENISM

Though not a "professional ecumenist," Merton articulated principles of genuine ecumenism with simplicity and clarity as evidenced in these excerpts from his letters to Marco Pallis and Etta Gullick as well as in the longer selection from an essay written in 1965 and reprinted in Mystics and Zen Masters *(1967).*

One must cling to one tradition and to its orthodoxy, at the risk of not understanding any tradition. One cannot supplement his own tradition with little borrowings here and there from other traditions. On the other hand, if one is genuinely living his own tradition, he is capable of seeing where other traditions say and attain the same thing, and where they are different. The differences must be respected, not brushed aside, even and especially where they are irreconcilable with one's own view.

— Letter to Marco Pallis, Easter 1965, HGL 469

•

To me it is enough to be united with people in love and in the Holy Spirit, as I am sure I am, and they are, in spite of the sometimes momentous institutional and doctrinal differences. But where there is a sincere desire for truth and real good will and genuine love, there God Himself will take care of the differences far better than any human or political ingenuity can. Prayer is the thing, and union with the suffering Lord upon His Cross. . . .

— Letter to Etta Gullick, November 24, 1966, HGL 378

•

Genuine ecumenism requires the communication and sharing, not only of information about doctrines which are totally and irrevocably divergent, but also of religious intuitions and truths which may turn out to have something in common, beneath surface differences. Ecumenism seeks the inner and ultimate spiritual "ground" which underlies all articulated differences. A genuinely fruitful dialogue cannot be content with a polite diplomatic interest in other religions and their beliefs. It seeks a deeper level, on which religious traditions have always claimed to bear witness to a higher and personal knowledge of God than that which is contained simply in exterior worship and formulated doctrine. In all religions we encounter not only the claim to (divine) revelation in some form or other, but also the record of special experiences in which the absolute and final validity of that revelation is in some way attested. Furthermore, in all religions it is more or less generally recognized that this profound "sapiential" experience, call it gnosis, contemplation, "mysticism," "prophecy," or what you will, represents the deepest and most authentic fruit of the religion itself. All religions, then, seek a "summit" of holiness, of experience, of inner transformation to which their believers — or an elite of believers — aspire because they hope, so to speak, to incarnate in their own lives the highest values in which they believe. To put it in grossly oversimplified language, all religions aspire to a "union with God" in some way or other, and in each case this union is described in terms which have very definite analogies with the contemplative and mystical experiences in the Christian, and particularly the Catholic, tradition....

Obviously, the dialogue conducted by theologians and bishops on the level of doctrine and of practical adjustment can never have any serious meaning if, in the background, there persists a deep conviction that the non-Christian religions are all corrupted in their inner heart, and that what they claim as their highest perfection and their ultimate fulfillment is in fact nothing but a diabolical illusion. However, I do not think that serious scholars and theologians are really making such sweeping generalizations today.

The Second Vatican Council in its Declaration on Non-Christian religions clearly recognized the validity of the "profound religious sense" which has enabled men of all races and peoples to recognize God, "to contemplate the divine mystery and express it," and to seek liberation from the anguish of the human condition. "The Church rejects nothing which is true and holy in these religions," says the Council, and it adds that the purpose of dialogue should be to combine "the sincere witness of Christian faith with the understanding and indeed preservation and promotion of the spiritual and moral goods found in other cultures." However, the Church in no way abandons her claim to announce the definitive message of salvation to the world in Christ; dialogue, as the Council conceives it, is not merely based on the assumption that all religious truths are equally and indifferently good. Nevertheless, supernatural contemplation is certainly admitted as possible in all religions....

Since in practice we must admit that God is in no way limited in His gifts, and since there is no reason to think that He cannot impart His light to other men without first consulting us, there can be no absolutely solid grounds for denying the possibility of supernatural (private) revelation and of supernatural mystical graces to individuals, no matter where they may be or what may be their religious tradition, provided that they sincerely seek God and His truth. Nor is there any *a priori* basis for denying that the great prophetic and religious figures of Islam, Hinduism, Buddhism, etc., *could have been* mystics, in the true, that is, supernatural, sense of the word.

On the other hand, everyone is aware of the opposite tendency, to loose and irresponsible syncretism which, on the basis of purely superficial resemblances and without serious study of qualitative differences, proceeds to identify all religions and all religious experiences with one another, asserting that they are all equally true and supernatural and differ only in the accidentals of cultural expression. To adopt this view as axiomatic would from the very start guarantee that the interfaith dialogue would end in confusion.

These two extreme *a priori* views, one which denies non-

Catholic religious experience all claim to validity, and the other which asserts that all religious traditions are equally true and supernatural in all respects, both proceed from a superficial consideration of the evidence. They are both oversimplifications. Certainly, a deeper and more serious form of research (and such research is beginning to make its results available today in works like those of R. C. Zaehner) will open the way to more qualified solutions.

But the fact remains that as long as the dialogue proceeds merely between research scholars and concerns only the objective study of documents, it will lack its most essential dimension. It is here that we see the need for the Christian contemplative to enter the discussion, in his own modest way, and for the non-Christian contemplative to enter it also.

Here, unfortunately, we are faced with many problems. Contemplatives are by the very nature of their vocation devoted to a somewhat hidden and solitary mode of life. They are not normally found on transoceanic jet planes, though their occasional presence there is by no means excluded. On the other hand, they are far more likely to be living in obscure places, without the benefit of any publicity, and known only to very few. It is also true that they may sometimes lack scholarly and theological preparation, and may indeed have absolutely nothing to say about their inner experience. Or they may, for various reasons, prefer not to speak about their spiritual way and about their tradition, being aware that such information is easily abused and that publicity might tend to falsify and corrupt it. There are, nevertheless, more and more scholars who are not only experienced in their own contemplative traditions, but have had an opportunity to visit monasteries where other living contemplative traditions are still flourishing.

Within the last two or three years, the Abbey of Gethsemani has been visited by men experienced and fully qualified to represent such traditions as Raja Yoga, Zen, Hasidism, Tibetan Buddhism, Sufism, etc. The names of some of these would instantly be recognized as among the most distinguished in their field. Therefore, the question of contacts and actual communication between contemplatives of the various traditions no longer presents very great obstacles. A little experience of such dialogue shows at once that this is precisely the most fruitful and the most rewarding level of ecumenical exchange. While on the level of philosophical and doctrinal formulations there may be tremendous obstacles to meet, it is often possible to come to a very frank, simple, and totally satisfying understanding in comparing notes on the contemplative life, its disciplines, its vagaries, and its rewards. Indeed, it is illuminating to the point of astonishment to talk to a Zen Buddhist from Japan and to find that you have much more in common with him than with those of your own compatriots who are little concerned with religion, or interested only in its external practice.

The reasons for this may be manifold, and one is not entitled to jump to rash conclusions. Nevertheless, however one may explain the fact, one may find in all races and in all traditions both the capacity for contemplative experience and the fact of its realization even on a very pure level. This capacity and this realization are therefore implicit in all the great religious traditions, whether Asian or European, whether Hindu, Buddhist, Moslem or Christian.

— "Contemplation and Dialogue," MZM 204–9

FROM COMMUNICATION TO COMMUNION

Shortly after his arrival in Asia in autumn 1968, Merton participated in the first "Spiritual Summit Conference" of the Temple of Understanding. The following is an excerpt from a talk he gave at that conference. Describing himself as "a marginal person," Merton invites his listeners to experience the deepest level of communication that is communion.

First, let me struggle with the contradiction that I have to live with, in appearing before you in what I really consider to be a disguise, because I never, never wear this (a clerical collar). What I ordinarily wear is blue jeans and an open shirt; which brings me to the question that people have been asking to a great extent: Whom do you represent? What religion do you represent? And that, too, is a rather difficult question to answer. I came with the notion of perhaps saying something for monks and to monks of all religions because I am supposed to be a monk....I may not look like one.

In speaking for monks I am really speaking for a very strange kind of person, a marginal person, because the monk in the modern world is no longer an established person with an established place in society. We realize very keenly in America today that the monk is essentially outside of all establishments. He does not belong to an establishment. He is a marginal person who withdraws deliberately to the margin of society with a view to deepening fundamental human experience. Consequently, as one of these strange people, I speak to you as a representative of all marginal persons who have done this kind of thing deliberately.

Thus I find myself representing perhaps hippies among you, poets, people of this kind who are seeking in all sorts of ways and have absolutely no established status whatever. So I ask you to do me just this one favor of considering me not as a figure representing any institution, but as a statusless person, an insignificant person who comes to you asking your charity and patience while I say one or two things....

I stand among you as one who offers a small message of hope, that first, there are always people who dare to seek on the margin of society, who are not dependent on social acceptance, not dependent on social routine, and prefer a kind of free-floating existence under a state of risk. And among these people, if they are faithful to their own calling, to their own vocation, and to their own message from God, communication of the deepest level is possible.

And the deepest level of communication is not communication, but communion. It is wordless. It is beyond words, and it is beyond speech, and it is beyond concept. Not that we discover a new unity. We discover an older unity. My dear brothers, we are already one. But we imagine that we are not. And what we have to recover is our original unity. What we have to be is what we are. *already*

— "Thomas Merton's View of Monasticism"
(informal talk delivered at Calcutta, October 1968), AJ 305–8

BETWEEN EAST AND WEST

Merton developed the theme of real communication, or communion, in notes for the second talk he had prepared to give at the Temple of Understanding conference in Calcutta in October 1968. Reflecting on intermonastic communication, Merton formulated principles relevant to all interreligious dialogue.

There is a real possibility of contact on a deep level between this contemplative and monastic tradition in the West and the various contemplative traditions in the East — including the Islamic Sufis, the mystical lay-contemplative societies in Indonesia, etc., as well as the better-known monastic groups in Hinduism and Buddhism....

We can easily see the special value of dialogue and exchange among those in the various religions who seek to penetrate the ultimate ground of their beliefs by a transformation of the religious consciousness. We can see the point of sharing in those disciplines which claim to prepare a way for "mystical" self-transcendence (with due reservations in the use of the term "mystical").

Without asserting that there is complete unity of all religions at the "top," the transcendent or mystical level — that they all start from different dogmatic positions to "meet" at this summit — it is certainly true to say that even where there are irreconcilable differences in doctrine and in formulated belief, there may still be great similarities and analogies in the realm of religious experience. There is nothing new in the observation that holy men like St. Francis and Shri Ramakrishna (to mention only two) have attained to a level of spiritual fulfillment which is at once universally recognizable and relevant to anyone interested in the religious dimension of existence. Cultural and doctrinal differences must remain, but they do not invalidate a very real quality of existential likeness....

On this existential level of experience and of spiritual maturity, it is possible to achieve real and significant contacts and perhaps much more besides. We will consider in a moment what this "much more" may be. For the present, one thing above all needs to be emphasized. Such dialogue in depth, at the very ground of monastic and of human experience, is not just a matter of academic interest....

I am convinced that communication in depth, across the lines that have hitherto divided religious and monastic traditions, is now not only possible and desirable, but most important for the destinies of Twentieth-Century Man.

I do not mean that we ought to expect visible results of earth-shaking importance, or that any publicity at all is desirable. On the contrary, I am convinced that this exchange must take place under the true monastic conditions of quiet, tranquility, sobriety, leisureliness, reverence, meditation, and cloistered peace. I am convinced that what one might call typically "Asian" conditions of nonhurrying and of patient waiting must prevail over the Western passion for immediate visible results. For this reason I think it is above all important for Westerners like myself to learn what little they can from Asia, *in* Asia. I think we must seek not merely to make superficial reports *about* the Asian traditions, but to live and share those traditions, as far as we can, by living them in their traditional milieu.

I need not add that I think we have now reached a stage of (long-overdue) religious maturity at which it may be pos-

sible for someone to remain perfectly faithful to a Christian and
Western monastic commitment, and yet to learn in depth from,
say, a Buddhist or Hindu discipline and experience. I believe
that some of us need to do this in order to improve the quality
of our own monastic life and even to help in the task of monastic renewal which has been undertaken within the Western
Church....

The question of "communication" is now no longer fraught
with too great difficulties. The publication of classical Asian
texts and of studies on them, especially in English and in German, has led to the formation of what one might call an
intertraditional vocabulary. We are well on our way to a work-
able interreligious lexicon of key words — mostly rooted in
Sanskrit — which will permit intelligent discussion of all kinds
of religious experience in all the religious traditions. This is in
fact already being done to some extent, and one of the results of
it is that psychologists and psychoanalysts, as well as anthropol-
ogists and students of comparative religion, are now able to talk
a kind of lingua franca of religious experience. I think this "language," though sometimes pedantic, seems to be fairly reliable,
and it is now at the disposition of theologians, philosophers,
and plain monks like myself.

This is a first step only, but it is an important step — which
will often have to be completed by the services of an interpreter.
He in his turn will be more helpful if he knows the "common
language," and is interested in the common pursuit of inner
enlightenment. Incontestably, however, this kind of communication cannot get far unless it is carried on among people who
share some degree of the same enlightenment.

Is it too optimistic to expect the monks themselves to make
this contribution? I hope not. And here we come to the "something more" that I referred to above. True communication on
the deepest level is more than a simple sharing of ideas, of
conceptual knowledge, or formulated truth. The kind of communication that is necessary on this deep level must also be

"communion" beyond the level of words, a communion in authentic experience which is heard not only on a "preverbal" level but also on a "postverbal" level.

The "preverbal" level is that of the unspoken and indefinable "preparation," "the predisposition" of mind and heart, necessary for all "monastic" experience whatever. This demands among other things a "freedom from automatisms and routines," and candid liberation from external social dictates, from conventions, limitations, and mechanisms which restrict understanding and inhibit experience of the new, the unexpected. Monastic training must not form men in a rigid mold, but liberate them from habitual and routine mechanisms. The monk who is to communicate on the level that interests us here must be not a punctilious observer of external traditions, but a living example of traditional and interior realization. He must be wide open to life and to new experience because he has fully utilized his own tradition and gone beyond it. This will permit him to meet a discipline of another, apparently remote and alien tradition, and find a common ground of verbal understanding with him. The "postverbal" level will then, at least ideally, be that on which they both meet beyond their own words and their own understanding in the silence of an ultimate experience which might conceivably not have occurred if they had not met and spoken...

This I would call "communion." I think it is something that the deepest ground of our being cries out for, and it is something for which a lifetime of striving would not be enough.

The wrong ways that are to be avoided ought to be fairly evident.

First of all, this striving for intermonastic communion should not become just another way of adding to the interminable empty talk, the endlessly fruitless and trivial discussion of everything under the sun, the inexhaustible chatter with which modern man tries to convince himself that he is in touch with his fellow man and with reality. This contemplative dialogue must be reserved for those who have been seriously disciplined by years of silence and by a long habit of meditation...those who have entered with full seriousness into their own religious community — besides being open to the tradition and to the heritage of experience belonging to other communities.

Second, there can be no question of a facile syncretism, a mishmash of semireligious verbiage and pieties, a devotionalism that admits everything and therefore takes nothing with full seriousness.

Third, there must be a scrupulous respect for important differences, and where one no longer understands or agrees, this must be kept clear — without useless debate. There are differences that are not debatable, and it is a useless, silly temptation to try to argue them out. Let them be left intact until a moment of greater understanding.

Fourth, attention must be concentrated on what is really essential to the monastic quest: this, I think, is to be sought in the area of true self-transcendence and enlightenment. It is to be sought in the transformation of consciousness in its ultimate ground, as well as in the highest and most authentic devotional love of the bhakti type — but not in the acquisition of extraordinary powers, in miraculous activities, in special charismata, visions, levitation, etc. These must be seen as phenomena of a different order.

Fifth, questions of institutional structure, monastic rule, traditional forms of cult and observance must be seen as relatively secondary and are not to become the central focus of attention. They are to be understood in their relation to enlightenment itself. However, they are to be given the full respect due to them, and the interests of dialogue and communication should not be allowed to subvert structures that may remain very important helps to interior development.

It is time to conclude. The point to be stressed is the importance of serious communication, and indeed of "communion," among contemplatives of different traditions, disciplines, and religions. This can contribute much to the development of man at this crucial point of history. Indeed, we find ourselves in a crisis, a moment of crucial choice. We are in grave danger of losing a spiritual heritage that has been painfully accumulated by thousands of generations of saints and contemplatives. It is the peculiar office of the monk in the modern world to keep alive the contemplative experience and to keep the way open for modern technological man to recover the integrity of his own inner depths.

Above all, it is important that this element of depth and integrity — this element of inner transcendent freedom — be kept intact as we grow toward the full maturity of universal man. We are witnessing the growth of a truly universal consciousness of transcendent freedom and vision, or it may simply be a vast blur of mechanized triviality and ethical cliché.

The difference is, I think, important enough to be of concern to all religions, as well as to humanistic philosophies with no religion at all.

> — "Monastic Experience and East-West Dialogue,"
> AJ 311–17

SPIRITUAL WAYS TO UNITY

The fundamental way to unity is spiritual. In this essay, published in 1965, Merton elaborates on what he calls "the poorer means" to unity — silence, prayer, fasting, and almsgiving — all of which "imply a more complete surrender to God."

There is no need to regret that a movement, providential in our day, is also suddenly fashionable. That Christians should be so openly and so actively concerned over Unity after four centuries of struggle, suspicion, bitterness, and intransigeance is without doubt a relief to everyone: a relief that can be fittingly celebrated by meetings and dialogues, with full publicity and exhaustive comment.

True, the popular press is always sweeping and superficial. It may tend to give a more triumphant evaluation of the advance toward Unity than is really justified. It tends to ignore the seriousness of obstacles that may remain confronting us for a long time. Yet there is a general feeling that we can now freely admit something that we have secretly desired all along, but did not dare to desire openly lest we invite humiliation, rebuff, and loss of face.

There is a general and well-founded sense that the Churches are no longer adversaries. At least this much has been achieved, and almost miraculously achieved. So it is right that there be meetings. That the highest dignitaries should embrace one another, without hypocrisy, that this should be seen and known, and that many should be moved by it to love one another where before they only feared and distrusted, perhaps despised, one another.

In a word, there has been an admission, a confession, of sin — the sin of division, for which all sides have been to blame. We see, with shame and sorrow, to what extent our forefathers allowed themselves to be blinded by a "noonday devil" of intolerance and self-righteousness. We begin to be aware of what great harm this division has done to the Gospel in the vast continents that did not know Christ. So it is right that now the sin be meditated by theologians and by whole Churches, and that the slow, painful work of healing and expiation be begun.

If this is celebrated in the press, and if now "the thing to do" is to engage in dialogue with someone, and if the gestures of friendship are multiplied, very well. They can be both public and sincere. And they must certainly be public, for this has been a public sin, a universal scandal. It is Christ whom we have torn with our petty refusals, our standing upon our dignity, our institutional arrogance, our relentless and intransigeant demands.

And yet, there are serious differences which must remain, and problems that have no apparent solution. There are on all sides values and truths that cannot be abandoned. They perpetuate division and difference, and yet to abandon them would also be an infidelity to truth and to that call to higher Unity, the way to which is still completely hidden and obscure.

For we cannot build true Unity on a casual indifference to essential values.

So, while there must indeed be displayed the splendor of large, visible, and successful methods, we must remember that these will not do all the work that has to be done. It is a work not of negotiation only, not of discussion, diplomacy, and theology, but above all sacrifice, suffering, expiation, prayer.

Let us then remember that the most important of all the means to Unity remain the poorer means, the hidden means, the ones which are accessible to all; and most of all perhaps to those without special talent, office, or mission. There is a greater mission, the mission of all, to pray and offer sacrifice, perhaps in total obscurity, the left hand not knowing what the right is doing.

The poorer means are those which, first of all, seldom or never have any clearly visible result.

They are, in fact, quite often the invisible counterpart of the visible and "splendid" means which are acclaimed and wondered at. For while the bishops and theologians have their mission to speak, and make declarations, to say where the ecumenical movement is going — indeed to *know* where it should be going, there are so many others who will not have anything to say, for whom there will be no dialogue that has any kind of importance, who will not know where it is all going, who will understand neither the questions that are being asked nor the answers that are being proposed. They may even be completely bewildered by the whole thing. They may fear for religious values which they know, in their hearts, to be completely authentic, indeed in some sense irreplaceable.

(For instance there has always been in the Church of England a special note of respect for the dignity of the personal conscience, and this is something born of no "revolt" but on the contrary, rooted in the most authentic Catholic and monastic part of Anglo-Saxon and medieval England — the clear-eyed and care-free England of Rolle and the Yorkshire hermits, of the author of the *Cloud,* of Lady Julian, of Chaucer's people, of Ailred of Rievaulx or the monk hermits and recluses who lived in the shadow of St. Albans Abbey.... It seems to me that the Caroline poets and divines assumed a certain noble responsibility, a risk not without anguish — and who cannot share and respect in his heart the anguish of Donne? — a risk, that, in its awful purity, could not but involve deep humility. One can say that T. S. Eliot's *Little Gidding,* or the Christmas of his Becket reflect this spirit and this humility. This is an austerity and beauty which Anglicanism cannot relinquish. Hence let it be clearly said that the Roman Catholic now needs to understand, at least obscurely, that the Anglo-Catholic repugnance for what seems to him an excessive and arbitrary authoritarianism is not a matter of perversity and self-will but indeed of serious principle. Yet at the same time the Anglo-Catholic will be aware of the opposite danger — the awful readiness of certain Anglican writers and speakers to jettison the most fundamental theological principles and engage irresponsibly in frank agnosticism in order to meet the spirit of the times!)

So, then, in closing this parenthesis, let us reflect that the first of the poorer means to Unity is *silence.* While there must be talk, and dialogue, there must also be the silence of those who cannot, or do not, participate in any discussions. This silence is a necessary counterpart of the dialogue, and it must be realized for what it is: an implicit admission that all cannot be said, and that agreements are not perfectly possible, and that all the answers are not within our grasp. Discussion that does not arise out of this silence and depend on it for strength, will be illusory.

The silence, even of those who are uneasy, or who do not understand, is therefore a guarantee of wholeness and hon-

esty in our ecumenism. And it bears witness to the helplessness
of man, and to our need for God. It reminds us of our total
dependence on Him for any result that is to have genuine
value.

Let us therefore not imagine that we must all have something
new and important to say, as if we knew the answers, whether
pessimistic or hopeful! We must remember that this is God's
work more than it is ours, and that it must proceed according
to a hidden plan that will not be revealed to us all at once,
but only in the measure that our silent expectation merits the
"word" that will tell us what step to take next.

This silence must not however be the mere dumbness of the
disconcerted. It must be turned to God in wakeful hope. It must
be a religious silence of listening and of beseeching, in which
the simplicity of the poorest and most humble prayer reaches
out to Him, not presenting Him with projects He must fulfil,
but waiting on His time and His initiative.

Another of the poor and universal means is *prayer*. Not only
the official and public prayer of Churches and congregations,
but the earnest prayer of the faithful in their own heart. Here
one might mention especially the Psalms, as a prayer of anguish
and sorrow, of repentance and longing for Unity.

> He took them from darkness and from gloom,
>   he snapped their chains.
> Let them thank the Eternal for his kindness
> And for the wonders that he does for men;
> He breaks the gates of bronze, and shatters iron bars.
>   Psalm 107:14–16

> O Thou Eternal, our God, save us,
> Gather us out of the nations
> That we may give thanks to thy sacred name
> And triumph in thy deeds of praise.
>   Psalm 106:47

"O Thou, who hearest prayer,
All men shall come to thee.
Though our sins be too much for us
'tis thine to cancel our transgressions."

Psalm 65:2–3 (Moffat translation)

In a very special way, *meditation* and *contemplation* are fruitful for Unity, since in them the Christian leaves the dispersion and distraction of everyday life and sinks down to deeper unity within himself, by the quieting of passion and fantasy, the putting off of self, and the complete willingness to obey God without reserve. In meditation, in contemplation above all, man is poor. (Those who think that meditation and contemplation are perhaps grand and special have perhaps not meditated much themselves.) In meditation man is reduced to nothing before God. He puts away all his projects and fancies, his self-ideal, his silly complacencies, his imaginings about achievement in the world, in order to become completely what he is — a thing of God, a property of God.

To silence, prayer, meditation, and contemplation as "poor means" we can also add that other characteristic form of religious poverty which is *fasting*. But with fasting also goes almsgiving, and here we come out again into the open field where action can be possible and visible. In our alms, whether spiritual or corporal, let us now think of those who belong to other Churches or to no Church — of those whom we would perhaps not normally think of helping. And here of course it can no longer be a mere matter of sixpence in the blindman's cup, or a guinea to the hospital fund. There are whole races asking to be fed, to be taught, and to be lifted up.

There is a certain aspect of poverty in those works in which members of different Churches cooperate together, renouncing any special glory or prestige for their own institution.

And there are also all the poorer works, in which men demonstrate together for the cause of peace....

The expression "poorer means" is inspired by *"les moyens pauvres"* of Louis Massignon, the Islamic scholar whom Charles de Foucauld brought back to the faith and who was such a devoted apostle of fraternal unity between Christians and Moslems. For him, the "poorer means" were certainly not restricted to a purely hidden and personal use. He conceived them in a context of conscious ecumenical Unity. His followers, Christian and Moslem, throughout the world join in days of prayer and fasting (usually the first Friday of the month) and sometimes go on pilgrimages together — Massignon had a special appreciation for the reverent practice of visiting the tombs of Moslems and praying for their dead, particularly for Algerians slain in the riots and violence of the fifties in France.

We have seen one main reason why the poorer means are most important and most powerful: they imply a more complete surrender to God, a greater delicacy of faith, a deeper appreciation of honest differences, a renunciation of concern with results, a more profound humility and purity of heart. They look more to God than to man's ingenuity and effort. They rely more on His mercy than on our own generosity, and yet they are in their own way most generous.

There is another reason which is historical.

It can be said that ecumenism in its deepest and most living form has been born in the trenches and barracks of wars and concentration camps. Certainly the rich flowering of ecumenism in Germany was due in large part to the fact that pastors and priests were thrown together in destitution of the camps, worked and suffered together in the greatest deprivation, without any chance, humanly speaking, to accomplish anything. Yet it was here, by God's grace, that wonderful things were indeed accomplished and a new understanding, blessed by a new charity and a new humility, came to light.

The brotherhood and understanding which have brought to life such miraculous new hopes and fruitful efforts toward unity were certainly born of poverty, suffering, humiliation, degradation. Let us never forget that the ecumenical movement in its very origins is sealed with the sign of poverty.

Merciful Lord, who prayed that we might be one, who died that we might be one, show us the true path to Unity. Bless, we beseech you, the sincere, devoted efforts of the Churches and their Shepherds, to come together in one. Bless above all and enlighten our own hearts to know and understand the power of silence, prayer, and fasting, so that we may more perfectly obey your hidden and mysterious will by which alone we can become truly one. For the glory of the Father, in the Word, through the Holy Spirit. Amen.

—PM

UNITED IN PRAYER

As Thomas Merton called to prayer participants at the First Spiritual Summit in Calcutta in October 1968, he spoke of the need for a new language of prayer, grounded in the love that unites people and transcends the differences between them. His prayer celebrates the unity that already is and implores God's help in realizing that unity in our lives.

I will ask you to stand and all join hands in a little while. But first, we realize that we are going to have to create a new language of prayer. And this new language of prayer has to come out of something which transcends all our traditions, and comes out of the immediacy of love. We have to part now, aware of the love that unites us, the love that unites us in spite of real differences, real emotional friction... The things that are on the surface are nothing, what is deep is the Real. We are creatures of love. Let us therefore join hands, as we did before, and I will try to say something that comes out of the depths of our hearts. I ask you to concentrate on the love that is in you, that is in us all. I have no idea what I am going to say. I am going to be silent a minute, and then I will say something....

Oh God, we are one with You. You have made us one with You. You have taught us that if we are open to one another, You dwell in us. Help us to preserve this openness and to fight for it with all our hearts. Help us to realize that there can be no understanding where there is mutual rejection. Oh God, in accepting one another wholeheartedly, fully, completely, we accept You, and we thank You, and we adore You, and we love You with our whole being, because our being is in Your being, our spirit is rooted in Your spirit. Fill us then with love, and let us be bound together with love as we go our diverse ways, united in this one spirit which makes You present in the world, and which makes You witness to the ultimate reality that is love. Love has overcome. Love is victorious. Amen.

—Special Closing Prayer (offered at the First Spiritual
Summit Conference in Calcutta, 1968), AJ 318–19

Epilogue

✚

Life is on our side.
The silence and the Cross of which we know
are forces that cannot be defeated.
In silence and suffering,
in the heartbreaking effort to be honest
in the midst of dishonesty (most of all our own dishonesty),
in all these is victory.
It is Christ in us who drives us through darkness
to a light of which we have no conception
and which can only be found
by passing through apparent despair.
Everything has to be tested.
All relationships have to be tried.
All loyalties have to pass through the fire.
Much has to be lost.
Much in us has to be killed,
even much that is best in us.
But Victory is certain.
The Resurrection is the only light,
and with that light there is no error.

—Letter to Czeslaw Milosz,
February 28, 1959, CT 57–58

HE IS RISEN

Thomas Merton drafted "He Is Risen" as an "Easter homily" in September 1967. It was published in 1975 — with pages of Merton's text set as free verse and interspersed with pages of contemporary color photos — by Argus Communications. In this reflection on the meaning of Jesus Christ's resurrection, Merton explores what it means to be church and what it means to be Christian.

"He has risen, he is not here...he is going before you to Galilee" (Mark 16:6–7).

Christ is risen, Christ lives. Christ is the Lord of the living and the dead. He is the Lord of history.

Christ is the Lord of a history that moves. He not only holds the beginning and the end in his hands, but he is in history with us, walking ahead of us to where we are going. He is not always in the same place....

Christ lives in us and leads us, through mutual encounter and commitment, into a new future which we build together for one another. That future is called the Kingdom of God. The Kingdom is already established; the Kingdom is a present reality. But there is still work to be done. Christ calls us to work together in building his Kingdom. We cooperate with him in bringing it to perfection.

Such is the timeless message of the Church not only on Easter Sunday but every day of the year and every year until the world's end. The dynamism of the Easter mystery is at the heart of the Christian faith. It is the life of the Church. The Resurrection is not a doctrine we try to prove or a problem we argue about: it is the life and action of Christ himself in us by his Holy Spirit....

True encounter with Christ liberates something in us, a power we did not know we had, a hope, a capacity for life, a resilience, an ability to bounce back when we thought we were completely defeated, a capacity to grow and change, a power of creative transformation....

The risen life is not easy; it is also a dying life. The presence of the Resurrection in our lives means the presence of the Cross, for we do not rise with Christ unless we also first die with him. It is by the Cross that we enter the dynamism of creative transformation, the dynamism of resurrection and renewal, the dynamism of love....

The first obligation of the Christian is to maintain his freedom from all superstitions, all blind taboos and religious formalities, indeed from all empty forms of legalism....

The Christian must have the courage to follow Christ. The Christian who is risen in Christ must dare to be like Christ: he must dare to follow conscience even in unpopular causes. He must, if necessary, be able to disagree with the majority and make decisions that he knows to be according to the Gospel and teaching of Christ, even when others do not understand why he is acting this way....

Too many Christians are not free because they submit to the domination of other people's ideas. They submit passively to the opinion of the crowd. For self-protection they hide in the crowd, and run along with the crowd — even when it turns into a lynch mob. They are afraid of the aloneness, the moral nakedness, which they would feel apart from the crowd.

But the Christian in whom Christ is risen dares to think and act differently from the crowd.

He has ideas of his own, not because he is arrogant, but because he has the humility to stand alone and pay attention to the purpose and the grace of God, which are often quite contrary to the purposes and the plans of an established human power structure.

If we have risen with Christ then we must dare to stand by him in the loneliness of his Passion, when the entire establishment, both religious and civil, turned against him as a modern state would turn against a dangerous radical. In fact, there *were* "dangerous radicals" among the Apostles.

Simon the Zealot was a member of the extreme left wing

of Jewish politics, a would-be freedom fighter against Roman imperial rule.

If we study the trial and execution of Jesus we find that he was condemned on the charge that he was a revolutionary, a subversive radical, fighting for the overthrow of legitimate government.

This was not true in the political sense. Jesus stood entirely outside of all Jewish politics, because the Kingdom was not of this world. But his actions could be twisted to look like political revolutionism. And yet he was a "freedom fighter" in a different way. His death and resurrection were the culminating battle in his fight to liberate us from *all* forms of tyranny, *all* forms of domination by anything or anyone except the Spirit, the Law of Love, the "purpose and grace" of God....

We have been called to share in the Resurrection of Christ not because we have fulfilled all the laws of God and man, not because we are religious heroes, but because we are suffering and struggling human beings, sinners fighting for our lives, prisoners fighting for freedom, rebels taking up spiritual weapons against the powers that degrade and insult out human dignity....

The Gospel account of the Resurrection in Mark is very suggestive. Not only is the Resurrection the key and center of the Christian life, but our Easter experience often follows the pattern of the experience of the Apostles and other witnesses of the Resurrection. The experience of the holy women at the tomb gives us a typical example of the dynamics of Christian faith.

We often forget that in all accounts of the Resurrection, the witnesses started out with the unshakable conviction that Christ was dead. The women going to the tomb thought of Jesus as dead and gone.

They had only one thing in mind: to embalm his body. But there was a problem. The tomb was sealed with a stone too heavy for them to move. They did not know how they would find someone who would roll away the stone for them so they could come to his dead body.

Now this is a kind of psychological pattern for the way we too often act in our Christian lives. Though we may still "say" with our lips that Christ is risen, we secretly believe him, in practice, to be dead. And we believe that there is a massive stone blocking the way and keeping us from getting to his dead body. Our Christian religion too often becomes simply the cult of the dead body of Christ compounded with anguish and desperation over the problem of moving the immovable stone that keeps us from reaching him.

This is no joke. This is what actually happens to the Christian religion when it ceases to be a really living faith and becomes a mere legalistic and ritualistic formality. Such Christianity is no longer life in the Risen Christ but a formal cult of the dead Christ considered not as the Light and Savior of the world but as a kind of divine "thing," an extremely holy object, a theological relic....

When the holy women arrived at the tomb, they found the stone was rolled away. But the fact that the stone was rolled away made little difference, since the body of Jesus was not there anyway. The Lord had risen. So too with us. We create obscure religious problems for ourselves, trying desperately to break through to a dead Christ behind a tombstone. Such problems are absurd. Even if we could roll away the stone, we would not find his body *because he is not dead.*

He is not an inert object, not a lifeless thing, not a piece of property, not a super-religious heirloom: HE IS NOT THERE. HE IS RISEN.   —HIR

MODERN SPIRITUAL MASTERS SERIES

Other volumes in this series are available at your local bookseller
or directly through Orbis Books.

Eberhard Arnold
Writings Selected with an Introduction by Johann Christoph Arnold
ISBN 1-57075-304-0, paperback

Dietrich Bonhoeffer
Writings Selected with an Introduction by Robert Coles
ISBN 1-57075-194-3, paperback

Charles de Foucauld
Writings Selected with an Introduction by Robert Ellsberg
ISBN 1-57075-244-3, paperback

Anthony de Mello
Writings Selected with an Introduction by William Dych
ISBN 1-57075-283-4, paperback

Henri Nouwen
Writings Selected with an Introduction by Robert A. Jonas
ISBN 1-57075-197-8, paperback

Pierre Teilhard de Chardin
Writings Selected with an Introduction by Ursula King
ISBN 1-57075-248-6, paperback

Oscar Romero
*Reflections on His Life and Writings by Marie Dennis,
Renny Golden, and Scott Wright*
ISBN 1-57075-309-1, paperback

Simone Weil
Writings Selected with an Introduction by Eric O. Springsted
ISBN 1-57075-204-4, paperback

For a free catalog or to place your order with Mastercard
and VISA, call toll-free 1-800-258-5838,

E-mail via our Web page at http://www.orbisbooks.com

or write to: **ORBIS BOOKS**
Walsh Building, P.O. Box 308
Maryknoll, N.Y. 10545-0308

Thank you for reading *Thomas Merton.* We hope you enjoyed it.